MW01290787

BEING SMART
ABOUT
CONGREGATIONAL CHANGE

DIANE L. ZEMKE, PHD

Copyright © 2014 Diane L. Zemke
All rights reserved
ISBN: 1494246376
ISBN-13: 978-1494246372
Cover Image: Shutterstock
Cover Design: Steven Zemke

for Steven

CONTENTS

INTRODUCTION

Some of you opened this book because you are in a congregation in decline, which, in reality, won't live another decade or maybe even a few more years. Everyone is grieving, angry, and fearful and you want to know what you can do to help.

Others of you may be in a congregation embedded in a denomination undergoing dramatic conflict over theology and practice. That conflict rolls down into the congregation each week, where it washes over everyone and impacts their relationships and ability to worship. You want to be able to survive and still minister in or to your community during the changes.

Or, perhaps you are in a congregation deeply afraid of societal changes where the solution has been to develop an unhealthy fortress mentality. You want to help open some doors to ministering to those around you.

Still others of you might be in a congregation that is inward-looking and complacent, where it seems everyone is happily asleep. You long to see your congregation grab hold of faith and ministry and make a difference.

Or, perhaps the manifestations of change in your congregation don't resemble what you were told in seminary. Everyone's looking to you for guidance and you don't really know where to start.

Maybe some of you are in new congregations, wanting to get a good start, but unsure of what that means. *Being Smart about Congregational Change* was written to give you the tools you need to enact change in your congregation.

When I first began writing this book I was focused on explicitly teaching change agents (a term used for a person trying to enact change) how to be effective at initiating change and survive while doing it. During my PhD research I had learned from several skilled change agents about how to survive and thrive while actively pursuing congregational and denominational change. I wanted to make their extensive wisdom available to change agents everywhere. Change agents, especially Protestant change agents, can be quite isolated and I wanted to create a playbook, if you will, for them to draw on. I wanted change agents to know there were others like them out there and offer wisdom and sustaining practices for them as they walked through change initiatives. Yet as I shared topics from that early draft with pastors, staff, lay leaders, and people in the pew it became obvious that everyone in a congregation struggles with change, not just change agents. Indeed, change agents are just one part of the larger dance of change in a congregation. They can't dance well without pastoral and lay partners. When these partners are missing or don't know the steps, change falls apart. It was also clear to me that everyone, even those thwarting change, had the best interests of the congregation at heart, but few knew how to act wisely. Nearly everyone I talked with, whether leader or laity, lacked a basic understanding of how congregations and change interact. These experiences helped create the current book.

So many of the books (and seminars) on congregational change are actually targeted toward congregational renewal or transformation. We're a success and growth-driven culture and that perspective is central to how we understand our congregations. Good congregations grow large and poor congregations don't. Good leaders grow big congregations and poor leaders don't. The entire conversation around congregational change centers on growth in numbers and finances and fixing whatever is wrong with your congregation so that it can *succeed*.

Yet congregational change is about so much more than growing in numbers and finances. It's more than renewal. Congregational change is about starting well, creating a healthy and faith-filled culture, bringing on staff, discerning direction, managing disagreement, enduring grief, and welcoming different perspectives. It's also about what to do when renewal is not a valid option, which is the hardest type of change to work with. This book is my attempt to shift the conversation, at least a little, toward wisely enacting change, toward being *smart* about it, whatever that change may be. This shift is important because congregations everywhere are immersed in change but not all are immersed in classic renewal strategies. Learning to be smart about change leads toward congregational health in any environment.

To give you the tools you need to be smart about change I've drawn on insights from organizational and leadership studies as well as knowledge from religion and spirituality. Each of these disciplines has much to say about change. Unfortunately, those skilled in one area are often ignorant of the wealth in the others. If we're to be smart about change in congregations we need to access wisdom from all of these disciplines and create a holistic practice of working with change. To that end, I've united these rich streams of wisdom to generate some fresh perspectives and practical approaches for enacting change in any congregational setting.

What to Expect

Being Smart with Congregational Change is written as a handbook, with a short review and exercises at the end of each chapter. My goal is to help you become smart about enacting change in your congregation, no matter what your congregation is like and no matter what kind of change you're pursuing. I've divided the book into three sections:

> ➢ Section 1 addresses the unique aspects of congregations. You can't be smart about change if you don't understand your congregation.
> ➢ Section 2 provides information on various facets of change. You need to clearly understand change if you're going to succeed.
> ➢ Section 3 explores how change agents, those enacting change, can care for themselves and each other.

SECTION ONE

BEING SMART ABOUT YOUR CONGREGATION

Thoroughly understanding your congregation is central to being smart about change. Many change initiatives fail because they haven't been tailored for the unique character of an individual congregation. We see an effective change strategy in another congregation or at work and try to bring it to our own congregation. Yet it doesn't succeed, people are upset, and we really don't know why. This section explores the unique nature of your individual congregation as well as why people can get so upset.

➢ Chapter 1 explores how the past creates the present.
➢ Chapter 2 reveals the distinctiveness of congregational life.
➢ Chapter 3 describes the influence of our corporate spirituality.
➢ Chapter 4 explains the impact of our shared story.
➢ Chapter 5 details the effects of a congregation's lifecycle.

1

THE PAST CREATES THE PRESENT

To those who are unfamiliar with the Church, most congregations seem the same. People get together, usually in a building set aside for meeting. They sing some songs about God, hear somebody talk about God, and pray to God. People give money and someone gives some announcements. Some people eat bread and wine. Everyone gets together afterward to chat and have snacks. This pattern can vary somewhat, but overall it is enacted every time congregations meet. To the outsider, everything seems pretty much alike. Differences in theology and practice have little impact.

To the insider, though, differences abound. Variations in Christian theology and practice dominate. Denominations are created and shattered on small differences in theology, interpretation, and practice. Yet to the insider of a particular denomination, it can seem that all the denomination's congregations should be the same. After all, everyone believes the same and has the same practices, usually determined by the denomination. One should be able to go to any congregation in the denomination and know what's going on and why. Everything should make sense and there should be no surprises. However, anyone who has been a member of two congregations in the same denomination, even in a denomination with a high level of control over congregational practice, will tell you he or she had some surprises, sometimes some really big ones. In reality, no two congregations are the same inside even though they may seem the same from the outside.

One of the reasons no two congregations are the same is because each congregation has its own culture. It has its own history, its own way of thinking about itself, its own way of living its life and passing it on. Denominational structures are only one, small facet of this culture. Indeed, it's possible to be more at home in congregations of differing denominations that embody a similar culture than in congregations in the same denomination with widely varying cultures. For example, two congregations can share similar values and make very similar choices in adapting to the society around them, even though their denominations differ. These two congregations will seem similar to someone coming from outside, even though some other structures may differ. People looking for a new congregation often find a cultural fit more important than a denominational one.

Understanding Culture

Like many terms, *culture* has several definitions. In this chapter we will work with one from Edgar Schein, an expert on organizational culture. He notes that within a group, culture creates a way of being together that is learned, shared, and passed on to new members. Culture enables group members to get along with each other since it defines appropriate behaviors. And, it enables the group to interact with the larger culture. [1]

There are a couple of key points in this definition that apply to congregations. The first is that everyone within the culture shares the same basic ways of thinking. Those who are unable or unwilling to share these basic ways of thinking will struggle and ultimately leave (or be asked to leave). These basic ways of thinking have less to do with denominational theology and more to do with how the group understands themselves and the world.

Second, culture is learned and develops over time. New congregations will have a weaker culture and more discussion (or fighting) about who they should be and what they should do. Established congregations have already made these decisions and have a more robust and settled culture.

Third, culture develops as congregational members grapple with how to make life work inside the group and choose how to interact with those outside. Some congregations fail here since they can't create workable ways of living together or what they're doing doesn't make sense to the larger culture around them and they fail to grow. Note that culture is created by what problems the congregation chooses to address, how they solve problems important to them, and what choices they repeat over time. It is not handed down from above or determined by the pastor, although a very long-term founding pastor will have an effect. Culture is developed and maintained by the congregational members.

Finally, culture is handed down without most people understanding that they are doing it. Culture becomes the way things are done. It's often invisible to those inside and they can be truly puzzled why newcomers (included a new pastor) have such a hard time and do such offensive things. After all, it's obvious what the right choice is, isn't it?

Congregational culture begins to form very early, often as soon as the second or third meeting. As soon as there are problems to solve and choices to make, culture starts to form and solidify. The problems the congregation chooses to address and the ones they choose to ignore also forms the culture. As the congregation continues to make choices, culture becomes more robust and more consistent since the group will tend to address many repeating problems the same way if that way worked before. People generally don't look for new ways to solve problems if they have a tried-and-true method. As the congregation becomes more established, these ways of solving problems and thinking about life can become very strong and hard to break.

Many factors work together to form a congregational culture. Understanding your congregation's culture is vital for enacting change since if change initiatives are to be effective they need to interact with, and make sense in, a given culture. Those asking for significant cultural change need to base the change within the current culture first and move forward from that point. Change initiatives based outside the culture are likely to fail since they violate basic assumptions and even seem incoherent to other congregational members. For example, urging an evangelical congregation to adopt mainline liturgical structures and written prayers may meet initial resistance since it violates congregational culture. Let's look at some primary factors that form congregational culture.

Generational Cohort

All congregations initially consisted of a small group of founders. Often, these founders, or what became the dominant group early in congregational life, shared the same generation. For example, many congregations were formed post-World War II by groups of young families. These founders had a worldview based on their experiences in the Depression and the war. These experiences caused these founders to create a congregational culture with particular values that resonated with their experience. Alternately, some congregations were formed during the 1970s. These founders had the experiences of the 50s and 60s to inform their choices. Congregations founded recently by young people will have worldviews informed by more recent events.

This situation is neither good nor bad, it just is. However, what is important to remember is that the choices and worldview of the dominant generation will persist over time. The congregational culture was created with the dominant worldview and it has been strengthened as the group continued to make choices. Thus, those congregations founded in the 1950s may have structures and beliefs that worked well in the 50s and 60s but are failing now. They will find moving forward difficult since they have 50 or more years of culture to rely on and may fail to see that these structures and worldviews no longer relate well to the present.

Geographic Location

Each congregation is founded somewhere as well as sometime. And those somewheres can have a large effect on the congregational culture. Rural congregations are more adapted to the change of seasons and the rhythm of planting and harvest. They also have had to adapt to a stable or declining membership with little opportunity for growth since few people move to rural communities. Members may have had to learn to live with each other creatively since other congregational choices are fewer. They may be more open to some ecumenical work since in a small town everyone attends everyone else's functions. The choices rural congregations have made and their approach toward enacting their faith will differ markedly from urban or suburban congregations.

The area of the country also has a large impact. In the Western US, church attendance is not as socially supported as in the Midwest or Deep South. In the West, you may be the only person in your neighborhood attending church regularly. A congregational culture created in an urban, secular environment may vary widely from that developed in a suburban, largely Christian environment, even within the same denomination.

Similarly, your congregation may be Roman Catholic in a largely evangelical area or evangelical in a largely mainline area. The congregation's problems and needs are different and the resulting solutions form the culture since one of the tasks of culture is learning how to interact with one's environment. If the environment is markedly different, the congregational culture embedded in it will be as well.

Denominational Issues

All denominations have issues they struggle with. Important current issues include sexuality, the role of women, worship styles, lay involvement, theological disagreements, how to respond to contemporary culture, and how to care for the poor. However, in the past there have been other important issues, such as civil rights, the role of education, divorce, and philosophical debates. Some of these issues have simmered for decades and others are wildfires that may split denominations and congregations. Some of these issues reside primarily in denominational headquarters and seminaries and others affect people in the pew every worship service. Denominational power and purity wars trickle down and individual congregations make choices on how to navigate them. Congregations make choices about how to address these issues that seem right to the group. They may align with denominational directives on one issue and choose to live in opposition as loyal dissidents on another. The congregation's choices in the early years affect the culture for the coming years. Earlier choices affect more current stances since members may see the present issue as part of a long-standing conflict.

Founding Circumstances

The founding circumstances of a congregation have a large impact on culture. Was the congregation founded from a church or denominational split? If so, the culture can perpetuate those old wounds and issues as well as a "we are better" attitude. It can fail to form a positive mission, instead focusing on what they are not.

Was the congregation founded as a grassroots group looking for a pastor and denomination? If so, the congregation may view pastors as employees, with the church council and members holding most of the power since after all, it's their congregation. They may also be less aligned with denominational interests or alternately, over-committed to them since they explicitly chose the denomination. Was the congregation founded as a church plant with a planting pastor? If so, people may be very attached to the founding pastor and have an easier relationship with the denomination, until it changes on them.

Was the congregation founded as a mission from a parent congregation? If so, they may still be closely attached. Alternately, they may be in a subtle (or not so subtle) competition. Understanding the founding circumstances also provides insight into how power is played out in congregational politics.

Economics

The economy has taken an enormous toll on people the last several years. Some research is showing that there are long-term negative effects for young people who have been unable to find work or work in their field. Similar effects have been reported for the long-term unemployed. Effects include depression, shorter lifespan, more unemployment in the future, less earning power in the future, and more pessimism overall.[2]

Those effects make their way into congregations. The economic times can affect how congregational members think about congregational finances. Do members worry over every last penny and argue over the price of toilet paper? Or do they take on debt and overspend? Those congregations founded with a Depression-era cohort, which had a similar economic situation as today, may struggle with spending for the life of the congregation. Alternately, those congregations founded when money was easier may face the world believing money will always be available. They may be more open to risk-taking but also struggle with meeting the bills even with good cash flow.

Ethnicity

Many congregations were initially founded as ethnic enclaves. For example, many Lutheran congregations began as Swedish, Norwegian, or German congregations worshipping in their native tongue. I have heard Lutherans talk about how their congregation was diverse because it welcomed other Scandinavian Lutherans rather than accepting only Swedes or Norwegians into membership! Similarly, some Roman Catholic congregations began as Hispanic, Italian, or Irish enclaves. Lutherans and Catholics aren't the only former ethnic enclaves. It is common and even healthy for immigrants to found a congregation where they feel at home and these ethnic enclaves may be the only safe and welcoming place for new immigrants.

However, a history as an ethnic enclave can cause problems later in a congregation's life. Some congregations can't move beyond their ethnic background even when everyone is fully acculturated and few new immigrants are arriving. Other congregations choose to enact their ethnic identity in unhealthy ways. To return to a Lutheran example, many Norwegian Lutheran congregations will host lutefisk feeds or bazaars featuring Norwegian baking. These events can be fun-filled and community-building as well as a way to welcome the congregation's neighbors. Or, the event can focus on who knows how to bake best and who has the best ethnic clothing with people being deadly serious about enforcing cultural practices. Sometimes the ethnic identity can override the Christian one.

A more subtle, but more far-reaching, effect is that different national or ethnic cultures view emotional display, gender equality, success, money, power, and leadership in different ways. For example, Northern Europeans are typically more emotionally reserved and their congregational culture will reflect this attribute. Those wishing more emotional warmth in worship may feel uncomfortable in these congregations. Alternately, those from a Northern European congregation may feel very uncomfortable in a congregation with high levels of emotional warmth, even though the denomination may be the same.

Opposing Views

I began this chapter with a definition of culture that focused on how groups learn to adapt and solve problems internally and externally. I have explored some of the major factors that form congregational culture. I would like to introduce another way of thinking about culture. Culture can be understood, not as a pattern of agreement, but as a continuing dialogue between opposing viewpoints. For example, in American politics, there is a constant discussion of states' rights vs. federal control. There is a constant discussion of a more socialist approach to the social safety net vs. individual responsibility, and so on. Similarly, in reasonably healthy congregations, there will be some ongoing discussions and some ongoing disagreement about some foundational topics. Health does not mean everyone thinks alike (more on this later).

These long-term disagreements probably developed early in congregational life and the congregation continues to struggle with the issue. Perhaps the conversation is over differences in theology or denominational directives, or aspects of worship, or pastoral/lay roles. Maybe it's over Christian education or how to best serve the poor. Most long-term members innately know what these long-term disagreements are and where they align. But newcomers, including pastors, won't know until they step into the middle of a polarized argument. Those enacting change need to investigate what the opposing viewpoints are and how they arose. How hot are the topics? What is the history? How does the proposed change initiative fit into this larger discussion?

The take away

➢ Change initiatives need to connect somehow to the current congregational culture.
➢ Understanding different attributes of congregational culture will provide entry points for your change initiative.
➢ Understanding how the change initiative aligns with long-term disagreements may lessen conflict or provide allies.

Taking it further

➢ Using the factors listed above, map out your congregational culture.
➢ Are there factors unique to your congregation? If so, what are their effects?
➢ What factors are strongest? Why?
➢ What are the long-term opposing viewpoints in your congregation? Where do you align and why?
➢ How does your change initiative impact the congregational culture?

2

THE DISTINCTIVENESS OF CONGREGATIONAL LIFE

Business reigns supreme in American culture. Since business is what America is all about, business publishing is big as well. If you go into any book store there is a wealth of books on how to be successful, how to grow your business, and how to transform your business so it's more profitable. Other media are also full of business wisdom. Some of this content makes its way into congregational life since many lay leaders are also working in business. Congregational leaders know they're struggling and business wisdom seems an easy source for answers. The same pressures are true for pastors. Many of them have received scant training in creating and managing change, so business texts on change may seem like a godsend.

Some business wisdom can be quite helpful. For example, many congregations can use help on how to conduct productive meetings and manage finances effectively. However, other content is less effective or even counter-productive. The reason for this situation is that most congregations are not businesses driven by market forces and pursuing profit. Congregations are a different type of organization with different underlying assumptions and different goals. In this chapter we'll explore the actual nature of congregations and what that nature implies for change initiatives.

Congregations are Voluntary Associations

Christians don't tend to think of church as voluntary. The Bible strongly encourages us to be in some type of fellowship with other Christians, which for most people means attending church, at least occasionally. Those with a Roman Catholic background may have been explicitly taught that worship attendance was an obligation. Thus, church attendance is a source of guilt for many people. They know they should go, they should be involved, but they just don't do it. So when I talk about church being voluntary, it can seem a little odd since most Christians see church as obligatory in some sense. Yet the reality is, congregations are voluntary associations.

Voluntary associations have a common purpose and have general goals, a name, a ruling body, and members. People participate voluntarily, rather than being compelled, as is the case with employment. The majority of the work is done by volunteers, rather than a paid workforce.[3] Many non-profits, especially smaller ones, are voluntary since volunteers do most of the actual work. Trade groups, sport and hobby groups, and professional societies are also voluntary. And so are congregations.

Within congregations, the ruling council consists of volunteers. Worship services are largely the product of volunteers, even though the (paid) pastor preaches. The work and ministry of the congregation is carried out by volunteers, even though there may be paid staff to support or direct it. Often there is some tension in congregations about what constitutes voluntary service and what is paid, with musical performance and cleaning the church building being classic cases. That this question even arises demonstrates that congregations are voluntary. Further, it's possible to have a viable congregation without a paid pastor. It's not possible to have a viable congregation with a paid pastor and no parishioners (volunteers).

Voluntary associations differ markedly from market-driven businesses. Businesses are outward-looking and interested in meeting the needs of potential customers. Voluntary associations tend to be inward-looking and interested in meeting the needs of their current members. This tendency toward inwardness makes sense when you consider how voluntary associations work. People join voluntary associations to have their needs met, whether physical, social, emotional, or spiritual. If these needs aren't met, people will leave and have their needs met elsewhere. While this tendency can seem somewhat selfish, in reality why would you stay in a group for the long-term when it doesn't meet your needs? Thus, voluntary associations, as an entire class, work hard at keeping their members happy and meeting their needs. If they don't, the group disappears, so the stakes are high, especially for paid staff.

In congregations, this tendency drives the congregation to try and meet insiders' wants and needs over those of outsiders. Worship is geared toward current members and ministry often meets volunteer needs as much as the needs of those ministered to. This situation is one reason why congregations struggle with outreach. It's more important to keep a stable and happy group of insiders than foster change to potentially welcome outsiders, while making insiders uncomfortable.

In addition, leadership, authority, and power in a voluntary association are ambiguous. In business, it's very clear who is in charge. There are usually clear lines of reporting and everyone understands who to follow. Managers have the authority and power to support their position and to direct how the work is done. Obviously, this description is over-simplified, but essentially true.

However, in congregations, especially Protestant congregations, the volunteers hire the pastors and staff. Pastors, in particular, are keenly aware that while they may have spiritual authority, real power rests with the members. If pastors push for change too vigorously, the congregation will push them out the door. Further, there tends to be a fair amount of conflict within congregations regarding pastoral vs. lay control. The Bible doesn't provide much actual guidance on church governance, which is why in Protestantism structures vary. Within Catholicism, priests have the authority of the Vatican behind them. However, the volunteers still have enormous power, including the ability to be so unsupportive of, or antagonistic toward, the priest that he is moved elsewhere and a priest more sympathetic to parish concerns is brought in.

Thus, in congregations, when change initiatives are brought forward, who is in charge of managing them? What happens when a pastor wants substantial change and the people don't or the opposite? Since it's unclear, it's much more difficult to advance change and much easier to torpedo it by handing off the initiative to the party with the least power. Those with the least power then become frustrated and leave or become burned-out so the change initiative dies. The proposed change can also ignite latent power struggles, again short-circuiting the change initiative. Why engage in discomforting change when you can have a congregational or denominational war instead?

With this background, it's easy to see why business strategies for change may not be effective within a congregation. Getting customers and generating profit are strong motivations for change in business. If you don't keep up, you're out of work. But congregations are inward-looking instead and don't feel the same type of pressures, thus lacking a

15

strong motivation for change. Further, organizational change in business also depends on a typical business structure, including the activity of managers with the power and authority to manage the change initiative. Power and authority in congregations are ambiguous and change initiatives can easily be thwarted or ignored.

Clans and Bureaucracies

The effects of voluntary association are strong in most congregations. However, there are other organizational effects working as well. Kim Cameron and Robert Quinn,[4] among others, have developed a typology or classification system for all types of organizations. Each of these types has particular ways of thinking about the world, goals they are trying to meet, and methods for achieving those goals. What are effective behaviors in one class of organization will be viewed negatively and often censured in another class. Cameron and Quinn describe four types of organizations: adhocracy, market, bureaucracy, and clan. These four types of organizations are created by assessing how flexible a group is and how externally focused it is. The figure below portrays these different types of organizations.

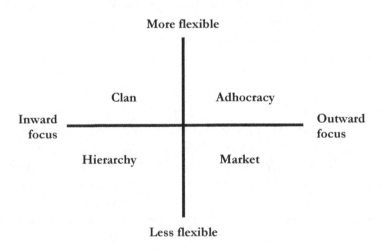

Figure 2.1: Four organizational types

Adhocracies can also be thought of as entrepreneurships. They are flexible and externally focused with few rules and policies. They easily adapt to changing conditions and are good at innovation. You can see why this type of organization would prosper in changing environments.

16

Most congregations are not adhocracies, although you sometimes will see it with a new, culturally adept congregation. However, as the congregation matures, it will move out of an adhocracy since this structure does not work well for congregations long-term.

Market structures are what we typically think of as for-profit businesses. Members are ambitious and competitive and initiative is highly rewarded. The goal is to serve the customer first and best so markets are very externally focused. The underlying goal is profit and growth. However, they are not strong in loyalty and trust, which is one reason why businesses have written contracts. The other reason is that contracts control the businesses' tendency to be totally self-serving.

Bureaucracies are the third organizational type. While Americans view the term bureaucracy negatively, it is actually a useful type of structure. Another term for bureaucracy is hierarchy. If you have a situation where you need a high level of control over what happens, such as a factory line or the IRS, you want a bureaucracy. Bureaucracies have rules and policies, much of which are written down. They have hierarchies of control and function on obedience and discipline. They are inwardly focused on their task and how to best achieve it. They don't like questioning of authority or innovation and do best in unchanging environments since they adapt very slowly. In many ways they are the opposite of an adhocracy.

Clans are the final organizational type. They are characterized by tradition, common values, grooming of leaders from the inside, interdependence, loyalty, and an emphasis on community. People learn how to be part of the clan by being part of the clan, rather than by following rules. The goal is to take care of the clan's needs and sustain an ongoing community so they are inwardly focused. Clans can be more flexible than bureaucracies since they have a lot of local control, but they also adapt slowly since they rely on traditional approaches. Clans don't like competition and individualism so in many ways they're the opposite of a market.

Established congregations are usually clans. Congregations work hard at mentoring people in their faith and creating and sustaining community. They focus on the good of the group rather than on openly competing with one another. People are encouraged to be loyal and care for each other rather than looking out for themselves. Congregations rely on tradition, both in their faith and in how they engage with their external environment. This reliance on tradition and on keeping the community together means that congregations will struggle with implementing change.

To make matters more complicated, many clan-like congregations are embedded in bureaucracies. If your congregation is Catholic or mainline Protestant, you will have a bureaucracy overseeing and controlling your activities and structures. In this clan-bureaucracy structure, several necessary behaviors that are key for fostering change are viewed negatively. These behaviors include questioning of authority or methods (rather than trusting your superiors), innovating (rather than using the tried-and-true), taking initiative (rather than obedience), and using flexible approaches (rather than policies). Further, what may be acceptable to an individual congregation in a particular location will not be acceptable to the hierarchy in which it is embedded. Change initiatives that work well have responded to local conditions, from which the bureaucracy is shielded. These initiatives may be thwarted by pressure from above to conform to the hierarchy's values and practices.

Most business strategies for change depend on a market or adhocracy organizational type to function. The pressures of the market support an openness to change. Initiative and innovation are rewarded rather than viewed as an open threat. Questioning is the path to the future, not the road to hell. This reality means that much business wisdom regarding change will be ineffective. Excellent wisdom is available, but it needs to be adapted to a clan or clan/bureaucracy framework first.

Unclear Metrics for Success

Businesses are great at measuring what they do. They know how much they produce, what their profit margin is, what they spend on their employees, what their expenses are, and often what their competitors are doing as well. Thus, when they implement some type of change they can measure its success. Again, this picture is an oversimplification, but businesses use data to understand how they're doing and what to do next. Change initiatives are framed as ways to increase profits, manage risks, and improve performance.

However, for congregations, what does improving performance actually mean? And, if you develop a definition for performance that fits within a congregational framework, how do you measure it? Denominations try to measure performance by collecting data on the numbers and demographics of members and on cash flow, but congregations are more complicated and this data doesn't give a good picture. Unlike businesses, congregations use poorly understood strategies such as building community. They have complicated goals such as addressing social ills, and have hard to measure outcomes, such as, saving souls.[5] Performance on building community, social reform, and saving people are the true metrics congregations should use, but measuring them is problematic at best. We can't actually measure how many people are saved since God isn't giving out that data. Social reform is always tricky to measure since we have little control over how other people behave, especially over the long-term. And, while some congregations develop a high quality, vibrant community, many others do not but seem to survive anyway. Thus, the effect of change initiatives on the most important variables is hard to measure. Yes, more people may be coming and there may be more money, but what does that actually mean for the congregation and its members? Business data is usually clear-cut. Authentic congregational data is not. Thus, business metrics for success don't transfer well to a congregational setting.

The take away

> Business wisdom regarding change and high performance does not transfer easily or well into a congregational framework.
> Business wisdom must be adapted to a framework that lacks external motivation for change, is concerned about maintaining community over growth, and doesn't have authentic metrics to measure success.

Taking it further

> How does your congregation demonstrate that it is a voluntary association?
> How is your congregation's true power structure ambiguous? Where do the tensions lie over power and authority and why?
> Develop a description of your congregation based on the clan framework. How well does it fit? What attributes from the other organizational types does it exhibit?

➢ What authentic measurements could you develop to reveal the success of your change initiative? Why have you selected these measurements? How would you obtain this data?

3

PRACTICING OUR FAITH TOGETHER

Spirituality is a hot topic in American culture. It appears frequently in
TV, movies, and other media. It's common to hear people claim they're
spiritual but not religious. People collect spiritual practices from many
sources and create a spirituality they feel comfortable with, often
outside of any religion at all. And, it's easy to engage people in talking
about their spirituality, unlike talking about religion. Spirituality is
everywhere in society, while religion, aside from election years, is less
visible.

Spirituality seems less visible in congregations than in society
overall. Denominations have often ignored spirituality, instead
emphasizing doctrine and theology. Until recently, few seminaries
offered training in spirituality, even from a Christian point of view. In
many congregations the topic of spirituality is often met with ignorance
or discomfort. Yet deepening or altering spirituality is often *the*
presenting issue in change initiatives, with attempts to develop a more
passionate spirituality a hallmark of renewal strategies.[6] Thus,
understanding the interaction of spirituality and change is central to
wisely enacting many change initiatives.

Spirituality 101

Spirituality is a very slippery term with many definitions. Evan Howard
maintains there are three main ways of thinking about spirituality.[7]
First, spirituality can be thought of as an academic discipline that
studies how people live out their relationship with God. Second,
spirituality can be understood as a way of describing how our
relationship with God works. For example, there is Franciscan
spirituality based in the life and teachings of Francis of Assisi. There is
Ignatian spirituality, evangelical spirituality, Celtic spirituality, and

Lutheran spirituality, to name just a very few. Each of these descriptions portrays how people should and do relate to God within those theological frameworks. Finally, spirituality refers to how we live out, in practice, our relationship with God. What do we actually *do*? How do we pray? How do we worship? What else do we do? Why? Some definitions of spirituality take this idea of practices a little further and explore spirituality through the lens of activities like prayer, fasting, and spiritual reading.[8]

These ways of defining spirituality can apply to all types of spirituality, Christian and non-Christian, so Howard also defines Christian spirituality. In Christian spirituality God is revealed through Jesus, the Bible, and the Holy Spirit. God is a living reality that can be known personally. We can communicate with God and God with us. And, this relationship is based in love. Thus, Christian spirituality is Christ-centered, Spirit-led, and expresses love.[9] If one of these facets is missing you may have a workable spirituality, but it won't be a Christian one. It's important to note this definition of Christian spirituality is still quite broad since it must encompass all of Christianity, from simple house churches to highly structured institutions, along with a host of other differences.

With this broad understanding of Christian spirituality, it's obvious that different denominations think about and embody spirituality differently. Some denominations may emphasize the work of the Holy Spirit more than others. Some emphasize knowing God through serving the poor while others may not. Other groups may pray using written prayers while others pray "from the heart." Thus, even with explicitly Christian spiritualities, there can be a lot of legitimate variation.

People switching denominations are usually aware of at least some of these differences since different denominations enact worship and communal life differently. Other differences are more subtle and take time to understand. Further, spirituality and congregational culture are intertwined. Each reinforces the other. Thus, even within a single denomination, spiritual practices and attitudes toward those practices can differ between congregations. For example, how a congregation chooses to observe Easter or Christmas is affected by its spirituality as well as its culture. To illustrate further, one congregation may choose to have a formal high church liturgy for Easter while another may choose a more simple service, even though both congregations are in the same denomination.

While spirituality can seem less visible in many congregations since it's not talked about much, in reality it's everywhere. If you view spirituality through the lens of practices, you are surrounded by it. All congregations pray, hear God's word, and care for others, to name just a few practices. How congregations (and members) enact these practices reveals a lot about their spirituality. Understanding how spirituality is embodied in your congregation is vital for wisely enacting change because many change initiatives directly affect spirituality.

Since spirituality is such a broad topic, I've chosen to emphasize two aspects in this chapter that seem most important when enacting change. The first is learning how to identify your congregation's dominant spirituality and how it interacts with change initiatives. The second aspect is how mainline Protestant spirituality is constructed and how it interacts with common renewal strategies. For those of you not in mainline Protestantism, my hope is that this example can reveal issues that you need to learn about in your own congregation before enacting change.

Understanding Your Congregation's Spiritual Type

A congregation's spirituality is affected by how the majority of members relate to reality. Corinne Ware, based on work by Urban Holmes, has developed a way of explaining different types of Christian spirituality.[10] These types can be applied to individuals and congregations. Indeed, if you are feeling in conflict with your congregation, especially over worship and spirituality, the root of that conflict may be a mismatch of spiritual types between you and your congregation. Understanding the characteristics of different spiritual types and where you fit in (or don't) can enable you to function more wisely and effectively when introducing change initiatives.

To begin, Ware draws two perpendicular lines. The vertical line represents a continuum of thinking and feeling. When you think about those you know well, it's obvious that some are drawn more toward thinking and some more toward feeling as they move through life. Some want to make decisions based only on facts and others base decisions more on how they and others feel, or use intuition. This continuum is similar to what the Myers-Briggs personality assessment measures with their thinking/feeling scale.

The horizontal line represents a continuum of concrete and abstract ways of meeting God. Another way of thinking about this continuum is whether you believe God is mysterious or easy to know through one's senses. In short, how do you use your senses to know God? Are you more comfortable in sensory-rich environments with lots of words, music, ornate liturgies, sacraments, images, and so on? Or, is it easier to experience God in silence and simplicity, with much less sensory input? Again, different people will respond differently.

The intersection of the thinking/feeling line with the mystery/concrete line results in four quadrants, each defining a spiritual type. Using the figure below, let's explore how an individual or a group in each of these quadrants interacts with God and others.

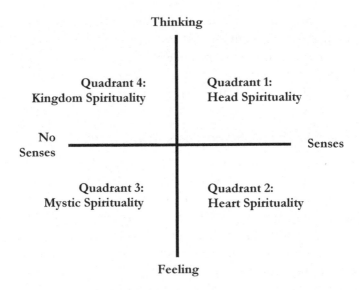

Figure 3.1: Four quadrants of spirituality

Quadrant 1 is known as "head spirituality." It ranks high on a tendency toward thinking and high on concrete, sensory ways of knowing God. Congregations in this quadrant focus on education and theological renewal. They have lots of Bible study groups, with study and doctrinally-focused sermon content a high priority. People work hard to know the Bible and theology well. Disagreements often appear as theological arguments about the correct interpretation of a text or belief statement. These groups tend to have a lot of order and structure in their lives together as well as word-filled liturgies.

Quadrant 2 is known as "heart spirituality." It shares Quadrant 1's emphasis on more concrete, sensory ways of knowing God, but ranks higher in feeling rather than thinking. Congregations in this quadrant are informal, with much less structure. They focus on witnessing, storytelling, and testimonials. People are interested in personally serving those in need. These congregations focus on personal renewal. Disagreements often appear as arguments over how to be holy and on right practice rather than right theology.

Quadrant 3 is known as "mystic spirituality." It shares Quadrant 2's emphasis on feeling but has moved toward mystery and less sensory input. This spirituality is characterized by the pursuit of simplicity, silence, and solitude. Worship is more contemplative and simple. People focus on hearing from God rather than talking to God. Mystic individuals often struggle with worship based in Quadrants 1 and 2 since these can generate sensory overload and there is little quiet time in more traditional forms of worship for hearing from God.

Quadrant 4 is known as "kingdom spirituality." It shares Quadrant 3's emphasis on mystery and Quadrant 1's emphasis on thinking. This quadrant focuses on social reform, obeying God, and witnessing to God's coming reign. Often individuals in this quadrant don't formally participate in a congregation although they remain Christian in belief. They would argue that many congregations are not deeply invested in social reform and congregations, overall, respond slowly. Thus, congregational life is frustrating and seems pointless to them. People in Quadrant 4 believe their action for social justice is their prayer. Quadrant 4 is the home of prophets, martyrs, and crusaders for social justice.

Most congregations will have a dominant quadrant for their spirituality, with small minorities from other quadrants. Ware argues that the path to spiritual growth for a group (and for individuals as well) is to begin to acquire practices from the quadrant that is diagonal (or opposite) to it. In contrast, what most people try to do is deepen and perfect what they are already doing when they should try to move out of their dominant quadrant, even in small ways. Thus, Quadrant 1 (head) would benefit from practices in Quadrant 3 (mystic). Quadrant 2 (heart) would benefit from practices in Quadrant 4 (kingdom) and so on. The goal is *not* to become more of what the congregation already is, but to expand its practices. Congregations should also work to appreciate its adjacent quadrants, which are often those it feels the most tension with.

For example, in a Quadrant 1 congregation, renewal strategies will often focus on having more Bible studies, more Bible-centered or doctrinally-centered preaching, and more education to move people forward. In reality, what the congregation needs for growth is experience in listening to God, based in Quadrant 3. Further, becoming more invested in testimony and social action will also help. This approach can seem counter-intuitive, since it appears to broaden rather than deepen. In reality, though, deeply investing in practices and assumptions that are already not sufficient is not a good strategy. Further, broadening the practices may bring in new people and new ideas, which can support change and renewal. It opens up the congregation to new ways of being Christian.

Ware notes that most congregations can't easily support all four quadrants. Each congregation should learn what quadrants make up the majority of the congregation and explore whether meeting minority quadrants' needs is important or possible in any meaningful way. Sometimes an alternative service will work as will adopting some alternative practices. Sometimes these options are not possible and congregations might consider how to bless minority quadrant members on their way out of the congregation toward one that is a better fit for them. However, leaders should understand that choosing to invest deeply in only one quadrant can generate unhealthy beliefs and practices over time. For example, focusing solely on doctrine and theology while ignoring serving the poor can create a spirituality that loses its ability to serve others well, which is part of the gospel.

If you are working to enact a change in spirituality but are in a minority quadrant in your congregation you should consider whether some of the tension you feel with your congregation arises from your minority status or from other issues. For example, if you are deeply investing in knowing God through enacting social justice and your congregation has practices that reflect a head spirituality, it might not be possible for you to find support for your way of knowing God. Nor will you be able to effectively bring aspects of your spirituality into the congregation. You will be frustrated and the congregation may actively oppose your efforts. If you choose to enact change coming from a minority quadrant it would be wise to find some group that supports your spirituality so you can sustain your spiritual health as you attempt change.

Knowing your congregation's (and your own) spiritual type can enable you to wisely enact change. So can understanding the historical and theological underpinnings of your congregation's or denomination's spirituality. As we move toward exploring spirituality in mainline Protestantism, I hope that some of the issues raised in the following discussion can be applied to your own congregation.

Spirituality in the Mainline

Mainline denominations came into being during the Reformation and as later reform movements. Common mainline denominations include Episcopalians, Lutherans, Methodists, and Presbyterians. Joseph Driskill claims that all mainline spiritualities share some common characteristics that cross these denominational boundaries and theologies.[11] These characteristics deeply affect change initiatives in mainline congregations, especially those attempting spiritual renewal.

Within mainline spirituality, people believe that God loves us and offers salvation to all who believe, yet God is also transcendent. God is interested in the big picture but is not really involved in a believer's daily life. God has provided the overall direction and people are to enact it. Those in the mainline may not understand their faith as having a relationship with God since they believe God is not really interested in having a relationship but in God's work in the world. There is often little emphasis on the work of the Holy Spirit in sustaining one's faith. These beliefs contrast markedly with the more evangelical beliefs that God is near to us and through the Holy Spirit will provide daily guidance on how to live out our faith. Thus, the practice of praying for guidance and daily needs, relying on God to provide, which is very common in evangelical circles, is less common in the mainline.

Mainline spirituality has a strong emphasis on ethics and social action. God's work in the world is based on Jesus' call for reform, justice, and love, which is seen in the gospels. People in the mainline understand part of their spirituality as working for social justice since that is what God has called people to do. They take seriously the call to love one's neighbor, both individually and in reforming dysfunctional social systems. Thus, spiritual practices that are not linked with caring, social action, and ethics can make little sense in the mainline.

Christian history has had a strong effect on mainline spirituality. Initial reform movements within the mainline gave rise to Pietism. Pietism was a response to lax practices as well as a Christianity overly focused on doctrine and head knowledge of God rather than a loving response to God. Pietism's solution was to create rigid codes of behavior and accountability to address laxity as well as encouraging a more relational and emotional response to God. Mainline spirituality historically had a negative response toward Pietism and became antagonistic toward religious experience, emotion, and many spiritual practices that support a more rigorous practice. These negative reactions were coupled with weak theologies regarding spiritual growth. The result is that practices such as daily devotions, lay-led prayer groups, or attending to one's spiritual experience either make no sense or feel threatening. From a mainline view, these practices are not closely linked to loving one's neighbor and open the door for a rigid and unloving approach to Christianity and/or to a purely experiential and emotional spirituality, none of which find an easy home in the mainline.

The mainline is also committed to historical, textual, and critical methods for understanding the Bible, which means they view understanding biblical revelation as more based in reason, using scholarly methods. Analyzing the Bible as a text is acceptable, but a devotional reading, listening for the guidance of the Holy Spirit, often is not. Further, since it takes seminary training to study the Bible in a scholarly fashion, the laity does not lead Bible studies. Thus, lay-led devotional Bible studies, focused on meeting God in the text and enacting the Holy Spirit's guidance, common in evangelical circles, are not as common in the mainline.

One of the reasons I'm using mainline spirituality as an example in this chapter is that renewing congregational spirituality is a very common change initiative in many congregations, but is perhaps most common within mainline denominations. Congregational decline has deeply affected the mainline in recent decades and laity, pastors, and denominational leaders alike are eager for anything to stem the tide of decline. Deepening congregational spirituality is an excellent place to start. Unfortunately, pastors may have received little, if any, seminary training in spirituality. Members in mainline congregations often know little about spiritual practices either, even those arising from their own tradition. Indeed, they may more know about Eastern and New Age practices than those from their own history. Thus, laity and pastors are actively seeking Christian spiritual practices that can support renewal and look for examples of thriving congregations to emulate. Those congregations are often evangelical.

Mainline leaders and members know that evangelicals have a rich experience of frequent prayer, devotional Bible reading, higher lay involvement, and a relational approach to God, as well as other practices. Since evangelical churches are currently not experiencing the rates of decline seen in the mainline it's easy to attribute their current health to their spiritual practices rather than other factors. And indeed, many evangelical congregations will score higher on passionate spirituality scales. Thus, mainline members and some leaders are eager to bring in these practices to reverse decline.

However, this strategy doesn't work well and creates avoidable conflict. If your congregation authentically embodies a mainline spirituality, asking people to engage in practices that don't mesh with their theological and spiritual framework can be counter-productive. First, many mainline leaders and members are openly antagonistic toward evangelicals generally for a variety of historical and current issues. Introducing openly evangelical practices without a lot of dialogue can generate negative responses with leaders and laity alike. Second, actively encouraging more relational forms of prayer and devotional Bible reading makes little sense to people with a mainline spirituality. The underlying belief system doesn't support the practices.

Driskill does offer a number of excellent suggestions for deepening and broadening mainline spirituality. Some are anchored in spiritual practices of denominational founders, such as Luther's *Simple Way to Pray*. Others are based in Roman Catholic practices such as a prayer of examen or a practice of morning and evening prayer. Still others are more contemporary, such as relaxation exercises. But what is central is to understand and honor mainline spirituality as it is and anchor new practices within it rather than patching on practices directly from outside. Any new practices need to be carefully integrated into members' current spirituality and theology.

The take away

> Since spirituality is often a major issue in change initiatives, understanding how your congregation embodies its spirituality is vital.
> Mainline congregations may not welcome evangelical practices since their beliefs don't support them. Anchoring new spiritual practices within mainline spirituality will help.

Taking it further

> Using Ware's description of the four quadrants of spirituality, what is your quadrant? Now map your congregation's quadrant. How do you match your congregation?
> What other quadrants are also represented in your congregation? How does your congregation support those quadrants?
> What practices from other quadrants would your congregation be open to trying? Why?
> If your congregation is in the mainline, does it have a mainline spirituality? What factors are strongest?
> If you are not in the mainline, what can you apply to your own congregation?

4

WHAT STORIES TELL US

Everyone loves a good story. We love the characters and their challenges. We want to see what happens at the end. Whether it's a mystery, a romance, or a thriller, we begin to live in the world of the story. Media matters little since books, radio programs, TV series, and movies all create the same effect. Indeed, movie series such as *Harry Potter*, long-term TV series, or reality TV do so well, in part, because we need to know what happens to the characters. We'll invest a lot of time, money, and energy to find out. For many of us, the idea that we would be yanked out of a story in the middle, unable to finish, is a type of torture.

We're not only interested in fictional stories either. We tell our children stories about our own childhoods. If we're lucky we have extended family around us to keep family stories alive. We like to tell stories about our lives to others. We tell each other stories about what happened at work, what our kids did yesterday, and what we did over the weekend. In fact, if we know our coworkers well, we can often predict what stories we'll hear from them, for good or ill. We can become almost as invested in their stories as our own. Whether it's fiction or our own lives, we're surrounded by stories.

It's not just individuals and families who tell stories. Larger groups tell stories about themselves as well. Some of you may work for companies that tell stories about themselves as part of their training or at employee meetings. For example, Hewlett-Packard tells the story of its founders working away in a garage and how the company grew from that humble beginning. Other companies tell stories of triumphing over a challenge or meeting an important need. Like other groups, congregations also tell stories about themselves. Learning what those stories are and how powerful they are within the congregation is crucial for anyone interested in change.

The Power of Narrative

The small stories we tell about who we are and what we've done, told over and over, create larger, stronger stories. These larger stories are called narratives. Narratives form the foundation for the way we make sense of reality. They are closely linked with culture, each reinforcing the other. For example, the war stories the US Marine Corps tells strongly reinforce their warrior culture, which supplies new stories that deepen the Corps' narratives. These narratives support and strengthen everything the Marine Corps does. They would not be the Marines without them.

Narratives are much stronger than the small, individual stories. They deeply influence what we see and what we don't see, as well as what we believe about ourselves. Narratives inform our tastes, our relationships, and enable us to keep seeing life in a particular way. In short, they help generate and maintain our worldview. As they support our worldview, they become nearly invisible. Large cultures like the United States have many defining narratives that create an American worldview.

Another interesting aspect of narratives is that they don't necessarily have to be completely true to have power. Indeed, narratives often portray what we would *like* to be true rather than what *is* true. For example, your company may have a narrative that they are the only company capable of generating world-class solutions in the face of difficult odds. Or, they may refer to themselves as the best in their category. While there may be some data to support these narratives the business most likely did not survey its entire category worldwide. These narratives are aspirational rather than factual.

Let's use an illustration of the power of narratives. The US has long been a world power and we have a narrative about how strong and invincible we are. We tell many stories to ourselves that reinforce this idea, going back to our founding. For example, we were instrumental in winning World Wars I and II and no one can successfully breach our defenses. Then 9/11 happened. One reason why 9/11 was such a shock was that it violated our invincibility narrative. It was one of the very few foreign attacks on US soil that succeeded and it took a decade to find bin Laden. The US also has a narrative about how generous we are to other nations and how we are a good neighbor to the rest of the world. Another reason 9/11 was a shock was we had to acknowledge that some nations saw us very differently than we saw ourselves. Some other nations believe the US is rich and selfish. So, with 9/11, not only did we have to mourn those who died, we also had to deal with events that challenged important American narratives. We've spent years choosing how to respond.

Narratives are also at work in businesses. Corporate executives know that a company's narratives are vitally important. It's why they tell the stories they do during employee meetings. The Hewlett-Packard example of the founders in the garage tells HP employees a great idea is more important than humble beginnings and that hard work and ingenuity are the path to success. Wise CEO's also know that if they're going to change the company they have to root that change within the current narrative or it won't make sense to the employees. Many failed corporate change efforts are the result of not understanding and working with the existing corporate narrative. Indeed, some leadership scholars understand leadership as the ability to communicate and work with narratives rather than the ability to command others.

Congregations are much smaller than the US and large corporations. They have only a few narratives that create their worldview. As noted above, these narratives don't necessarily have to be completely factual to have power. Even though these narratives are smaller since the group is smaller, they can be just as strong as those in the larger US culture. As with corporations, change efforts need to be rooted within the existing narrative. Thus, surfacing a congregation's narrative becomes vital for success.

Congregational Narratives

James Hopewell was interested in the effect of narratives on congregations.[12] Initially, he set out to interview members of two mainline congregations (Baptist and Methodist) in the same town to discern what their congregational narratives were. He believed that each congregation would be unique and have its own distinct culture. If one wanted to learn about a congregation one should approach it just like an anthropologist approaches a new culture, because that's what it is. So he set out to observe what people did and asked them what they believed in order to understand their culture.

At first, Hopewell asked members about various denominational beliefs and theological statements. He found this line of questioning to be unfruitful in surfacing the narratives. What was fruitful was asking people to recount some personal crisis in their lives and inviting them to speculate about what was going on behind the scenes. Where was God in these crises? What was God doing? This line of questioning generated many revealing stories. Note that these narratives are not based so much on theology but on where and how people saw God acting in their lives. People consistently interpreted God's action one way and this way was reinforced, creating a narrative.

Hopewell was surprised by the responses. He had entered into his research believing that people existed on a spectrum ranging from belief and unbelief and on a spectrum ranging from liberal to conservative. He expected to sort people within each congregation along these lines. This predicted pattern was not the case. Instead, people fell into four major categories, primarily operating from one category with minor contributions from one or two others. The categories had little to do with belief/unbelief and liberal/conservative. Hopewell's findings seem to resonate more with Driskill's idea of the mainline spirituality I explored in Chapter 3.[13]

When Hopewell further expanded his study and analyzed his data, he found that each congregation primarily consisted of people holding the same type of worldview. To put it simply, most people in the congregation explained the action of God in his or her crisis event the same way. Sociologically, this result makes sense since people tend to cluster with others like themselves. As stories are told in a congregation, new people evaluate how they fit or don't fit into the larger narrative. Below is a very brief summary of Hopewell's four categories.[14] Keep in mind that Hopewell was interviewing practicing Christians. See if you can find your own worldview and that of your congregation.

➢ In a Canonic worldview, people rely on authorities interpreting God's revealed word or will, which they then obey. Thus, hearing and preaching God's Word or listening carefully to these authorities is central.

➢ In a Gnostic worldview people rely on a more intuitive understanding that the world is moving from chaos toward unity. People focus on obtaining enlightenment and wisdom.

> In a Charismatic worldview people rely on the experience of meeting God in their lives. God is a living actor in one's life and should be called upon to provide.
> In an Empiric worldview people rely on what they can understand through their five senses. In this worldview people believe you should be realistic about how things work and reject supernatural intervention.

As you consider these worldviews you should find one that you resonate with as well as others that seem odd. However, there are congregations and Christians that fit within each worldview. Each congregation's worldview will affect how it works with change.

Change and the Narrative

Hopewell also argued that a congregation will not violate its own narrative, even if it's in its best interest to do so. In other words, a congregation will not act in a new or different way that goes against its narrative even if it must do so to survive. Hopewell recounted working with a large, progressive Southern congregation to create an adult education course on racial equality and diversity.[15] Everyone thought the course was a great idea and many people signed up to attend. But when the first day of the course arrived, there were few attendees and attendance continued to dwindle as the weeks wore on. Why? Hopewell believed the course violated a key congregational narrative. This congregation had been a strong advocate for civil rights in its area and it saw itself as a hero in the fight. Yet the course material argued there was still work to be done in racial equality. The course topic violated the congregation's self-understanding of its historical role in the struggle for civil rights. In short, if the congregation had won the battle (and it believed it had), then why explore how to promote racial equality and diversity? It was threatening to the narrative and people refused to participate, even though they could not articulate specifically why.

I have seen this response in my own experience. For a time, I attended a congregation that was deeply declining. Many elderly members, still a strong force in the congregation, had attended for over 40 years. This congregation was the only one they had known and they were deeply invested in it. The pastor and leaders were struggling with how to graciously close and leave a legacy for new ministry since it was clear the congregation had no hope for renewal and could not persist at its current low level.

Twenty years earlier the congregation had hit a rough patch and the denomination had rescued it by providing financial support and a pastor/savior to pull them out of difficulty. At that time the denomination was financially healthy and the congregation was also larger, younger, and healthier. It still had much to offer. Based on this experience, a narrative developed in the congregation that the denomination would always rescue them if there was trouble. The denomination would financially support them and send them a pastor/savior to turn things around. The current reality was that the denomination itself was in serious financial trouble and that the congregation was in steep, unrecoverable decline. There would be no rescue. Yet it proved impossible to move people from the belief in the rescue. "They'll rescue us" became a mantra with this group. They refused to enter into planning for a different future or engage with the idea of leaving a legacy. The power of the rescue narrative prevented them from living in reality or entering into what God would have for them in the future. Their narrative thwarted change rather than supported it.

Listening for Stories

It's clear that narratives are important in congregations. Yet since narratives are often invisible to most of the congregation, you can't go up to people and ask them to explain what the congregational narratives are. Nor is asking them to describe the congregation very helpful either. People who like their congregation invariably say it's "friendly" and "welcoming" and they "feel at home." They may also offer that they like the preaching or the pastor or the music. Since everyone answers this way, it does little to surface the narratives you need to learn about.

However, since narratives are based in congregational experiences and stories, storytelling is a great place to start. In the congregation I discussed above, the pastor and leaders worked very hard to understand what narratives were blocking renewal and/or legacy planning. They hosted a Saturday all-church retreat where the congregation created a timeline of its history. Long-term members told stories of founding, of building, and of growth. They also told stories of conflict, pastoral failure, and grief. They told stories about God and

God's action in their own lives and in the congregation. This congregational history and its associated stories clearly revealed patterns and narratives, both in key individuals and in the group as a whole. This event was well-received by long-term members since it honored their experiences and work in the congregation. It provided rich understandings for the leaders. An alternate way of exploring the history would be to have small focus groups or one-on-one interviews with long-term members.

Another way to surface narratives is to look at the stories told in historical documents in the congregation. Many long-term congregations have had important anniversaries (50 year, 75 year, etc.) and have prepared booklets describing their history to those dates. Reading these booklets can be revealing indeed. Since narratives persist and become entrenched, you can see them develop over time. You can also see how the congregation implements the narrative. Similarly, reading a decade or two of annual reports is also revealing. Focus on the pastor's report and those of key committees. What challenges does the pastor highlight? What direction do the congregational leaders want to move? What happened the next year?

Still another way is to take a hint from Hopewell and treat your congregation as a new culture you are stepping into. Some of us can do this more easily than others, but try seeing everything with new eyes. What do people say about God's activity in their lives? What words do they use? Where was God during crises? What seems important to people? What does the bulletin highlight? What events happen? By asking these questions you may be able to surface at least some of the congregational narratives.

Surfacing narratives and working with them is a starting point for significant change initiatives. Narratives can support mission and ministry and reinforce core values. They can keep the congregation on track and healthy even in the face of trauma. Unfortunately, they can also make it very difficult to change, even when the congregation needs to. They can perpetuate unhealthy patterns and blind people to realities they need to pay attention to. Clearly understanding your congregation's narratives provides a good foundation for wisely enacting change.

The take away

➢ Stories are the way we make sense of reality. These stories create narratives that generate and maintain a congregation's worldview.

➢ Change initiatives need to be rooted within current congregational narratives.

➢ Congregations will not violate their narrative easily, even if it's in their best interest.

Taking it further

➢ What stories are important in your life? Can you identify at least one narrative that reveals who you are?

➢ Explore congregational conflicts in the past. What were the issues? Who was on which side and why? Was the conflict resolved? How?

➢ Meet with a long-term member of your congregation. What do they believe are some defining moments of the congregation?

➢ As you look at your change initiative, how might a dominant narrative interact with it? Will it support it or resist it? Why?

5

BEGINNINGS, ENDINGS, AND THE SPACE BETWEEN

All living things have lifecycles. They are born (or sprouted), they grow, mature, age, and eventually die. We are all very familiar with this pattern and familiar with the effects time has on living things. This pattern occurs with non-living entities as well. Institutions and organizations are born as very small groups or even ideas. They grow and become larger and more influential. As time moves forward, their growth and influence plateau. Eventually, the organization or institution dwindles and dies. This death can be a take-over, a closing, or a sale, but the organization, as it was originally conceived, no longer exists.

For example, in 1955 the Fortune 500 was created. It listed the top 500 companies in the United States by gross revenue. Since 1955, 1,800 companies have appeared on the list.[16] Today, of the original Fortune 500, less than 75 are still listed. Some big names, companies that seemed strong at the time, are gone: Bethlehem Steel, Zenith, Rubbermaid, Chrysler, and Scott Paper.[17] Perhaps the brand name still exists, but the business itself doesn't. Newer companies, often founded fairly recently (at least in terms of the Fortune 500) now appear: Wal-Mart, Microsoft, Apple, Google. And, given the current economic uncertainty, it's clear that there will be yet more changes in the list.

People are familiar with the idea of a lifecycle, both for living things and for organizations. Yet what people often don't consider is that congregations have lifecycles as well. They confuse language about the universal Church being eternal with their congregation lasting for centuries. They want to believe their congregation will last forever. Yet congregations, like people and like every other organization, have lifecycles. Change initiatives often arise out of particular life stages in the congregation.

Figure 5.1 is a model or idealization of a congregational lifecycle. Since it's a model, many different curves are possible, but this representation is a common experience. Note the *x* axis (horizontal line) measures time in terms of decades. Many congregations are declining after 60 or 70 years. The *y* axis (vertical line) measures congregational health. Congregational health includes not just the number of members and the size of the budget, but also aspects such as enthusiasm, types of ministry, quality of lay leadership, vision, and so forth. Many of these last aspects are less tangible, but give a more accurate indication of health. Also, note the dotted line, indicating renewal. Renewal is a possibility that can extend a congregation's life by decades, but it's not a given. This chapter will explore each stage of the congregational lifecycle and its interactions with change.

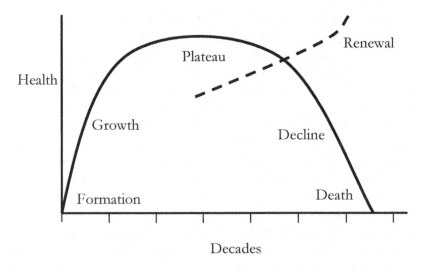

Figure 5.1: Example of congregational lifecycle

Formation

As I noted in the chapter on congregational structure, congregations are voluntary associations, where people come together to have important needs met. In the case of a congregation those needs include wanting to hear the Word of God preached, partake of the Lord's Supper, have fellowship with like-minded people, engage in mission with others, and provide for the spiritual nurture of children, among other needs. Congregations can be planted as a top-down mission from a denomination or larger congregation, a grassroots association of like-minded people, or result from the breaking up of a congregation. Each of these formation stories, as noted in the chapter on congregational culture, will have effects that resonate in congregational culture throughout the ensuing years. In particular, congregations founded as splinter groups, either from another congregation or as a refuge from denominational decisions, will have serious issues to address almost immediately. If they are to do well, they need to forgive those they have split from, avoid becoming a single-focus refuge, and develop a healthy identity rather than one based on "we're not them." These issues form a significant hurdle for these new congregations.

Grassroots and some top-down congregational plants form as a group of like-minded friends, which is also called a common bond group. Common bond groups, over time, don't do well since they are unable to manage conflict constructively. Conflict endangers relationships more easily since everyone is a friend, so people become conflict avoidant or leave if conflict occurs. Alternately, plants can form as a group that embraces a mission or new direction, which is also called a common identity group. Common identity groups have the possibility of managing conflict in more healthy ways and thus do better over time They focus on issues rather than on maintaining relationships or using relational pressure to solve problems.

There are few authentic change initiatives operating during formation since everything is new and hopefully adapting to meet internal and external needs. If the group is unable to adapt, it will not survive for long. If you are a leader in a new group, it's important to focus on creating a healthy, constructive culture since the culture will persist through the ensuing years.

Growth

Significant growth can occur almost immediately or it may be a number of years later. What causes a congregation to grow is its ability to create constructive ways of living together and constructive ways of interacting with those outside the congregation. The group finds a constructive way to meet God together and join in mission. If it fails on either of these tasks, it will fail to grow. If the inside culture is not functioning well, people may initially join, but then leave because they feel unwelcome, can't get inside the founding group, can't withstand ongoing conflict, or sense no true mission, among other reasons. If the congregation can't interact with its outer environment, people will not join since what the congregation is doing will seem incoherent or of little value. The goals of the congregation have to make sense to those outside. People need to believe that they can get at least some of their needs met by joining. If the congregation is unable to adapt to the outside, it will eventually die by attrition since founding members will die, age-out, or move.

Congregations founded from splits may struggle with generating authentic growth. Their initial growth was the result of people joining to align against their former group. Once all of the refugees have joined, the congregation may have no other mission than refuge. Or, it will only welcome those in complete agreement with the founding issues. Thus, they will struggle with welcoming new people and allowing them to enter leadership.

Growth is frequently a time of conflict in a congregation and how the congregation chooses to manage conflict also affects how it grows. The conflict primarily arises from two sources. First, as people come in, the congregation has to adapt how it's doing everything to accommodate the growth. For example, in small congregations most business is conducted informally and everyone feels like a family. As a congregation grows it needs to create more formal structures and policies. The need for formal structures and policies and the implied lessening of individual power and group intimacy can generate conflict. Some groups thus decide not to grow and informally lock new people out. If the group chooses this path, it will have a short life.

A second source of conflict is that new people bring new perspectives and different legitimate needs and desires to the congregation. The congregation needs to broaden its culture to accommodate some level of difference and learn to honor different viewpoints. Here again, some groups decide they can't accommodate others and again, informally lock new people out. This choice leads to a short life.

However, if the group does decide to grow, it will, along the way, strengthen and deepen its culture and its narratives. This result is good in that it means that most of the problems of being church are worked out so that more ministry can happen. This result is also a problem in that the congregation becomes less adaptable over time.

During growth, initiating change can still be fairly easy, especially if it is connected to the evolving culture and narrative. The congregation should still be somewhat flexible. And, while it can feel threatened by growth, if it has decided to grow changes that support more growth may be welcome. However, if a change initiative stresses an already stressed-out congregation, it may be better to hold off for awhile since people can accommodate only so much change at once.

Plateau

During plateau congregational life seems to ease up. Identity is strong so there is less conflict. All the mechanics of being church have been worked out so there is less conflict. People know who they are and what they're doing. The narrative is stable and continuing to deepen. Finances seem steady, even in the face of economic troubles. Numbers are fairly steady as well. There are strong lay leaders and perhaps the congregation has an extended ministry such as a preschool, afterschool program, or feeding program. Those leaders who served during the growth phase may finally feel like they can take a breath. Yes, each year will present its challenges, but they'll usually pale in comparison to the challenges of formation and growth. It's time to relax.

Or is it? If you return to Figure 5.1, you'll note that plateau can start a few decades into the congregation's life. Often it can be thirty years or more. And, it can last for several decades as well. By the time a congregation hits a mid-point plateau, it hasn't updated its mission for years if not decades. Indeed, the reason growth has leveled off is that the congregation is no longer working as constructively with its environment. It has also become more rigid and less willing to adapt.

Some here might argue that the Word of God is timeless, as is caring for one's neighbor. In one sense they're right. God's Word endures forever and we'll always have the poor with us. Yet if you consider the changes you have seen in your own life over 30 or 40 years, or the changes in American culture in that time, you can see why approaches to mission, narrative, and culture may need to be reexamined.

Let's use the role of laywomen in many congregations as an example. During the 50s and 60s many women did not work outside the home. However, they did work, broadly and deeply, inside congregations, even though they were often not allowed into formal leadership positions. They taught Sunday School, served the poor, ran large fundraising events, sang in choir, visited the sick, and served funeral meals. Much of congregational life was tightly structured around the voluntary service of these faithful women. However, today many women work outside the home. They don't have the time, energy, or interest in providing this level of voluntary service to the congregation. Wise congregations have adapted and adjusted their expectations, acknowledging that women can't provide this level of voluntary service.

Congregations in plateau face a crucial choice that portends how the rest of congregational life will go. Should they update their mission, revisit and renew their culture, and rework narratives to support growth? Or, should they continue on their course as is? Some congregations choose to reexamine mission. They realize that 30 or 40 years is a very long time, especially in our current dynamic environment and that their situation has changed dramatically, as have their members. Old structures and comfortable ways may feel easy, but they're no longer effective.

Or a congregation can choose to stay the course. Realistically, most congregations choose this path, often not realizing what the future will bring. After all, everything is working well, at least on the surface. Why fix it if it's not broken? However, choosing to maintain is to choose decline and eventually death.

Change agents tend to be more active during plateau. They seem to sense that life has gotten too easy and old ways are not working. However, if the congregation has chosen, often by default, to stay the course, most people will not be open to change. Change agents will suggest new ministries and new ways but be ignored or shut out.

Decline

Decline can start slowly. Maybe things feel increasingly stale or perhaps you notice attendance and giving has tapered off. At this point, most people think emphasizing evangelism, giving, and commitment will do the trick. Yet that doesn't work well and you notice only a slight improvement, which wears off quickly. Bit by bit the situation continues to worsen. Eventually, sometimes after a decade or more, decline really picks up steam. Suddenly the congregation can't make budget. It's laying-off staff. People are getting worried. Unfortunately, by this time, it's usually too late to recover, at least without a lot of trauma. The time to address decline was in plateau or very early in decline, often over a decade ago.

During decline, congregational health plummets. Numbers and finances dwindle, but so does enthusiasm. There is often little skilled lay leadership since they have either aged-out of the congregation or left in frustration after attempting various change initiatives. People desperately want young families, but treat them poorly when they come, not allowing them a seat at the idea table or the power table. They may reminisce about young children in the congregation but now complain about the noise and mess they create. People develop a strong focus on keeping the doors open rather than on ministry. Indeed, most ministry, outside of weekly worship, has ceased. The entire system feels deep threat, which makes the group rigid. Instead of experimenting with what might work, which could be a path toward renewal, the group clings tightly to the tried and true since it worked so well before.

Unfortunately, the tried and true is what got them into trouble. Decline is caused by what made the congregation so successful during growth: its culture. That culture may not have been revisited in perhaps 50 or 60 years. Similarly, its narratives, hopefully once a source of health, now often thwart change rather than support it. Although there may be some interest in renewal, if only to maintain the congregation, there are few institutional resources and little energy. Successful renewal efforts can take a lot of energy as well as taking a number of years to realize. The congregation no longer has the time.

Many change agents find themselves in declining congregations. If you are one of them, here are some perspectives to consider. Decline is the result of the *entire* lifecycle, not the fault of the people at the end. It is also difficult to address since by the time it's recognized, it's far advanced. You can't turn back the clock or roll the ball back uphill. Renewal or transformation efforts can work but their success rate is low and they actually take a number of years to enact.[18] Further, they really do transform the congregation, requiring massive outlays of energy and resources from a highly stressed system. If your congregation is largely elderly, it may not have the strength and flexibility for transformation. In short, congregational death is a true possibility and a good option if it can be handled well.

Death

Ironically, Christians are terrible about talking about death, especially the death of their congregation. Even when death is discussed in light of resurrection, it's not well-received and many people refuse to even consider that the congregation will die. Yet if decline can't be reversed, death is indeed the result. However, congregations can have a good death or a bad death. Sometimes wise change agents can make all the difference.

In a bad death, the congregation refuses to plan for its closing. People blame the current pastor, often in his or her first pastorate. They blame the lay leadership and the denomination. They blame the culture and the young people and everyone else. They stonewall any renewal initiatives and engage in magical thinking and change avoidance. In the end, which does indeed come, the money is spent, there may be significant debt, and people leave one by one, wounded and grieving. Some return to church only for their funeral.

However, in a good death, the congregation plans for its closing. The pastor and leaders focus on helping people name and work with their grief (read more on this later). The congregation investigates ministries that embody their values and makes plans to give their remaining resources to that ministry, carrying on a legacy. The leaders are proactive rather than reactive and create a workable timeline for closing. Caring continues until people are placed in new congregations and follow-up reunions are planned. The end, while sad, is also a time for acknowledging God's work in the life of the congregation and God's continuing work through the congregation's legacy. However, while a good death is a laudable goal, it is also a radical goal. Many congregations won't consider this option since it seems to be admitting defeat. In actuality it is recognizing reality and acting as a faithful steward of the gifts God has given the congregation.

Renewal

As stated above, renewal is an option. However, renewal does not just consist of a change here and a change there. It's not just about getting more contemporary music or updating the sanctuary or the constitution. At its heart, renewal is about reexamining and updating congregational culture and narratives. It's about sorting through all the pieces of the culture and narrative and deciding what can be kept and what must be adapted or left behind. It's very fruitful work and can extend congregational life by decades and open doors for new ministries. It's also difficult work, with a low rate of success. Renewal initiatives generate a lot of conflict. The congregation will lose people, money, and energy in the process. It may lose pastoral and lay leaders as well. And, it can take several years to implement. If you are a change agent pushing for renewal, remember that the earlier serious renewal efforts are begun the better. If your congregation is in deep decline, it's probably more realistic to work with people to prepare for a good death. Focus on caring for grieving people and creating a legacy of the congregation's ministry.

The take away

➤ All congregations have lifecycles. They are formed, mature, and close.
➤ Each stage of the lifecycle has specific issues that interact with change.
➤ Change agents are most active during plateau and decline.

Taking it further

➤ Where is your congregation in its lifecycle?
➤ If your congregation is in plateau, is it deciding to reexamine its mission or stay the course? Why?
➤ If your congregation is in deep decline, is it choosing to pursue a good death or a bad death?
➤ Are renewal initiatives practical for your congregation at its stage of life?
➤ How does your change initiative interact with your congregation's lifecycle?

SECTION TWO

BEING SMART ABOUT CHANGE

Being smart about your congregation forms a solid foundation. But you also need to be smart about change itself. Implementing change initiatives requires some distinct skills and perspectives to be successful. This section provides specific tools for working with change.

> ➢ Chapter 6 describes change as an adaptive process.
> ➢ Chapter 7 presents strategies for managing conflict.
> ➢ Chapter 8 reveals why dissent is actually positive.
> ➢ Chapter 9 explores the role of grief in change.
> ➢ Chapter 10 details the many pitfalls in decision-making.
> ➢ Chapter 11 explains the impact of commitment during change.

6

CHANGE AS AN ADAPTIVE CHALLENGE

Everyone has challenges in their lives that they deal with daily. Some of these challenges are fairly simple, such as needing to fix the muffler on the car. Other challenges are truly difficult, such as managing end of life care for a loved one. Between these two examples range challenges of varying complexity. Most people become adept at solving the simple everyday problems, but everyone struggles with the truly complex challenges. These complex challenges, when handled well, push people to adapt to a new way of living. Their identity, or who they are as a person, also changes as they incorporate what they have learned along the way.

Like people, organizations also have challenges and most of us are familiar with these from the workplace. As with personal challenges, organizational ones vary from those that are simple to those that are very complex indeed. For example, setting hours and pay for work may be a fairly simple problem while dealing with a drastic decrease in revenue is a very complex challenge. Since congregations are a type of organization one would expect to see varied challenges within them and indeed this reality is true. It's particularly true now, since congregations overall are struggling, some merely to survive. Congregational members can find complex challenges mounting faster than their capacity for addressing them. This chapter offers a way to think about working with difficult challenges within congregations and how to understand major change as a way of adapting to new ways of living together.

Three Types of Challenges

Ron Heifetz and his colleagues have spent much of their careers studying how to work with difficult challenges. This chapter will draw primarily on their work and adapt it to a congregational setting.[19] Heifetz argues there are essentially three types of challenges and knowing what type of problem you have is vital for addressing it well.

Technical problems are simple. It's easy to understand what the problem is and it's easy to understand what the solution is. Having a broken muffler is a technical problem. So is having a simple infection. In each of these cases, you can go to an expert or an authority (a mechanic or a doctor) and he or she will provide the solution (a new muffler or antibiotics).

Congregations have many technical problems and unless the congregation is functioning very poorly or struggling with severe budget shortfalls solving these problems is straightforward and causes little conflict. Examples of technical problems may include a replacing a roof, needing new office equipment, or lowering the utility bill. In each of these cases members can go to an expert and receive help or information that enables them to solve the problem. The roof is replaced, the office gets new equipment, and an energy audit is performed and acted upon. Outside expertise saves the day and most of the congregation will not need to change their behaviors or values.

Hybrid problems are more complicated. It's easy to understand what the problem is, but it's more difficult to create a solution. While you can still go to experts they are less helpful because you have to adapt their solution to your own life. For example, the doctor says you need to lose weight. It's easy to understand that your weight is causing problems and you agree with the doctor to work on losing weight. Yet how should you do it? You know you need to eat more wisely and get more exercise, but how you choose to do that is up to you. You must choose when and how to exercise and when and how to adjust your eating. Thus, while identifying the challenge is easy, the solution is not. You must change something inside yourself, rather than changing something outside yourself. You must adapt to a new reality, one of exercise and improved diet. As you adapt you will begin to change your values and your identity.

In congregations, hybrid problems are common as well. For example, you may want to start a new worship service to accommodate growth or changing needs. Everyone agrees with the solution, but making it work is more challenging. When should the service be? Will it be a traditional, contemporary, or contemplative format? Who will staff it and preach at it? These choices will also generate some conflict even in a healthy congregation since some people will lose, depending on what choices are made. They may need to come at a different, less convenient time or no longer be able to attend other functions that are important to them. Parking becomes more congested and the education hour(s) and music practice(s) may need to be moved. The entire congregation needs to adapt and its identity will shift a little as well as everyone accommodates the new service.

Adaptive problems are the most difficult type to address. In adaptive problems it's hard to understand exactly what the problem is and it's also difficult to generate possible solutions. Experts can provide information, but you must decide which information is helpful and which is not. They are of far less help since the solution to the problem resides completely within you. In adaptive problems, you must develop a new identity and learn to live with different constraints. For example, perhaps you have been out of work for a year and have no prospects in your chosen field. What should you do? Do you move to a different area? Do you retrain? If you retrain, what do you retrain in? Should it be something completely different or similar to your former work? How will you afford retraining? And, why are you unemployed and others in the same field are not? If you successfully address this challenge you develop a different identity and live in a different reality than before. The process is slow and generates a lot of soul-searching. Dealing well with adaptive problems means your life fundamentally changes.

In congregations, the classic example of an adaptive challenge is congregational decline. Why is the congregation in decline? Why aren't new people coming or staying? What should the congregation do? Should it change or keep on the same path? If it decides to change, how should it change? The solution to these problems resides within the group itself. While experts can provide some helpful background information they can't solve the problem. A weekend retreat doesn't work since these types of challenges can take many months or even several years to work through. Adaptive problems in congregations also generate enormous conflict since people are afraid of how they may need to change and feel they have a lot to lose. The way forward is not clear and group anxiety runs very high. Let's examine adaptive problems in more detail.

Adaptive Challenges

Heifetz argues that adaptive challenges are based in values and identity and affect the entire system. The foundational issue is that the group's values and/or identity must adapt to a changing environment if the group is to prosper. For congregations, this changing environment may include social changes, a changing neighborhood, an aging membership, denominational issues, and a host of other pressures. If the congregation is going to prosper in the future, it will need to reassess its current values and identity to see how they can be adapted to the current situation. While initially this reassessment may only occur at the council level, eventually it involves the entire congregation. This process is slow, generates conflict, and takes much personal and organizational energy.

Adaptive challenges are difficult, both personally and in organizations. Personally, adaptive challenges require much soul-searching as one reassesses values and constructs an identity that will prosper under new constraints. Organizationally, adaptive challenges surface latent value conflicts as identity shifts to accommodate a changing environment. As identity shifts people stand to lose relationships that are important to them. They also stand to lose power and status, both within the congregation and in the community. These potential losses fuel some very hot emotions, even among the most calm and reflective of members. This triad of value conflicts, shifting identity, and potential loss propagates across the congregation. Yet refusing to address adaptive challenges means that the congregation doesn't learn and grow. Over time it becomes ingrown and less effective. Eventually decline and death set in.

Let's look at an individual example of an adaptive challenge. If one visits with widows, most will tell you about learning to live a wholly different life upon the death of their spouse. They needed to establish new routines and their identity shifted as well. For many, this process was slow and took energy. While this process could be seen as part of grief (which we'll look at in a later chapter), this creating a new life is also an adaptive challenge. Yet we also know that some widows fail to make this leap. They are unable to create a new life and live constructively with a new identity. The same is true for congregations.

Recognizing an Adaptive Challenge

Most people fail to recognize that they are working with an adaptive problem and thus fail to work with it successfully. Identifying a problem as adaptive is the first step toward generating solutions. Heifetz identified several characteristics of adaptive problems.

First, in an adaptive challenge there is a history of seeing the problem as a technical one. People then use technical solutions or "fixes" and those technical fixes have failed. Most people are adept at technical fixes and since technical fixes work well and quickly, people initially turn to them for a solution. People like technical fixes since they require little internal change and are often fairly inexpensive. They create little conflict. Thus, the pull toward a technical fix is strong anytime there is an organizational challenge. People will usually identify any problem as technical and pursue technical fixes, at least initially.

For example, to return to the example of congregational decline, a technical fix would be putting up new signage or using social media to draw more people in. Another technical fix would be to slash the budget to the bare minimum to stanch the flow of red ink. A third fix would be to start an evangelism program. While all of these fixes may indeed be needed, they help only for a short time. A couple of new people come and the budget is more stable. Yet a year or two later, decline rears its head again. In fact, the underlying challenge has become more dire since the actual problem of decline was not addressed. Precious time and energy have been used that were needed to address the true, adaptive challenge. What the congregation needs to do is reassess its identity and focus on who it is in a changed world. The solution resides inside, not outside.

A second way to identify an adaptive challenge, closely related to the history of technical fixes, is that it will have a history of failed expert advice. Congregations struggling with adaptive problems often bring in outside experts for a weekend seminar or send a small group to a conference. The experts and conferences may provide excellent resources, but the congregation is unable to adequately use them. In an adaptive challenge, resources must be adapted to one's own situation. Expertise and authority located outside of the group and unfamiliar with the group's reality are of little use. Here again, the reason for the failure of experts is that the problem and the solution reside inside the congregation. It is the congregation itself that must change and the required change is specific and unique to the congregation.

A third type of adaptive challenge is ignoring the elephants in the room. Elephants are those topics, ideas, and issues that everyone knows are there, but can't openly discuss. At some point an agreement was made to actively turn a blind eye to avoid conflict. For example, in a congregation all significant council decisions have to be unofficially approved by a legacy leader, even though he or she is not currently in an official leadership position. This person will veto any decision not to his or her liking although the congregation overall may favor it. Surfacing backroom dealing and instituting clean leadership practices is an adaptive challenge.

Another common type of adaptive challenge is work avoidance. Work avoidance is when the group refuses to perceive the challenge as adaptive. Common work avoidance strategies include pursuing a technical fix even when past ones have failed, creating a personality conflict, taking some options off the table, or telling a joke or ending a meeting when the topic comes up. People can also displace responsibility for addressing the problem by marginalizing or scapegoating someone, attacking authority, or externalizing the enemy. All of these strategies take the group's attention away from the adaptive challenge and place it on other issues. Time and energy are diverted and often the group is worn down by the work avoidant behavior and doesn't return to addressing the adaptive problem.

Let's return to the example of decline to explore work avoidance a little further. Pastoral and lay leaders may have successfully identified decline as an adaptive challenge and started the process of reassessing identity. Yet as the issues become clearer, a segment of the congregation begins to attack the leadership as incompetent. Alternately, members of the council may refuse to consider some realistic options, effectively taking potential solutions off the table. Or, a substantial interpersonal conflict erupts in the congregation, diverting energy from working with decline. While it's true that leadership may not always be as competent as we would like and some options are indeed harebrained, wise leaders understand that these behaviors may be work avoidance events rather than legitimate concerns.

A final way to identify an adaptive challenge is by the type of presenting problem. Some classes of problems tend to generate adaptive challenges. One class of problems is the gap between stated values and enacted values. For example, a congregation may say that it welcomes all types of people into fellowship. In reality, members feel uncomfortable with people unlike themselves and isolate those who are from different cultures or socioeconomic classes. Aligning stated values with enacted values is an adaptive problem.

Another common class of adaptive problems is the inability to manage competing commitments. For example, the congregation may vow to give ten percent of its money to missions yet every month fails to do so. Other optional priorities intrude and the money is spent on those. Managing competing commitments is an adaptive problem. While on the surface it may seem that this alignment should be a technical fix, in reality it is adaptive since the issue is not budgetary, but is based in conflicting values.

Working with Adaptive Challenges

Successfully navigating adaptive challenges requires skillful leadership, both pastoral and lay. Each brings significant skills and roles to the issue and when pastors and lay leaders work together success is more likely. Let's look at some strategies that can help you move through adaptive challenges.

First, unless a problem is obviously technical, spend significant time reflecting on the actual nature of the problem. What values are involved? Will solutions affect the entire congregation in significant ways? Who will experience a loss of power, status, and/or relationships? How will the congregation be different as a result of moving through this challenge? Reflect on how your environment may have changed as well. Where are the disconnections between your congregation and its current environment? If the problem is indeed adaptive, clearly identify it as such to others.

Second, map the problem. For many adaptive problems there are small technical problems embedded within them. Solving these smaller problems quickly and easily can reveal more about the true nature of the adaptive problem. So, if your budget needs some modifying, do so, but don't expect the budget modifications to solve the problem of reassessing values. If you need new signage, do so, but again, don't expect it to address the adaptive problem. Addressing these smaller problems moves them out of the way so that you can attend to the real challenge.

Third, create an emotional space for working on the problem in the congregation. Most of us personally avoid adaptive challenges since they are difficult. Groups also avoid them. The key is to keep the issue in front of the congregation so that people feel enough urgency to work on the problem. It's important to keep the group anxious about the issue so they view it as important, but not so anxious that they give up or back away. Creating this space is the most important part of working with an adaptive challenge and the most difficult. Too little anxiety and nothing will happen. Too much anxiety and people quit or get discouraged. Members need to be actively engaged but not frantic.

Fourth, as people become engaged there will be an onslaught of proposed technical fixes. Leaders need to keep the focus on solving the adaptive problem, of reassessing values and identity. So, to return to the example of decline, the answer is not a new pastor, or new council members, or young families. It is not signage or the budget. It is the hard work of looking at the nature of the congregation and adapting its values and identity to its current environment.

Finally, one of the most common strategies of work avoidance is to attack the leaders. Adaptive challenges make people anxious. Worse yet, there is no clear path through, which also makes people anxious and angry. This mix can make pastoral and lay leaders a very easy target. Pastoral and lay leaders need to work together and protect each other publicly, even if they have private disagreements. Many people view it easier to attack leadership than to remain anxious as the group begins to reassess itself.

Adaptive challenges are difficult. They take personal and congregational energy. There is no clear path through and everyone must feel their way along. Yet the rewards are very great. When the adaptive challenge is met well, the congregation is renewed and ready for new avenues of ministry.

The take away

➤ There are three classes of problems: technical, hybrid, and adaptive. Technical problems are the easiest and adaptive the most complex.
➤ Adaptive problems involve reassessing values and identity. They generate conflict and the path forward is unclear.

Taking it further

➤ What is a technical problem your congregation is facing? A hybrid problem? An adaptive problem?

➢ What characteristics have led you to identify the problem as adaptive?
➢ Are you seeing work avoidant behaviors in the leadership or in the congregation? If so, what are those behaviors?

7

WORKING WITH CONFLICT

Wisely enacting change means becoming skilled in working with conflict. As several of the previous chapters have indicated, conflict is common during congregational change. The sources of conflict are varied. Perhaps your proposed change requires a change in congregational culture or introduces new spiritual practices and perspectives. Or, maybe the new path disrupts a long-standing narrative that members value and embody.

I have entitled this chapter "Working with Conflict," rather than "Avoiding Conflict." It's impossible to avoid conflict when enacting change. What is possible is to understand some sources of conflict, avoid some common pitfalls (both portrayed in the book's first section) and wisely choose the conflicts you do engage. Understanding your congregation is the foundation for enacting change and the potential for conflict.

As noted in the previous chapter, significant change is often an adaptive problem or challenge. Adaptive challenges, by their very nature, generate individual and group conflict because they require a change in values, identity, and ways of being for individuals and the group as a whole. For individuals, that conflict often manifests as deep soul-searching and a slow struggle to move forward. However, in a group, adaptive challenges are not manifested as everyone doing their soul-searching separately and quietly. The community works through the change *together* with people at different stages of problem-solving and embodying different, conflicting interests. And, to be honest, some people aren't interested in the process at all, instead engaging in a chorus that the change is pointless or wrong or downright sinful. This reality produces conflict in even the best circumstances.

Adaptive challenges spawn high anxiety in people since there is no clear path and most people and groups don't like to muddle through, at least for very long. They like a short and direct path forward to a clear and known goal. Further, reexamining one's foundational beliefs is deeply uncomfortable. Thus, the very process of adaptive change threatens many and some people will find it easier to generate open conflict rather than withstanding the ambiguity of adaptive change.[20]

Potential losses are also a source of conflict. At least some congregational members stand to lose relationships, power, status, or a way of life they value and many of them would rather fight than lose what is important to them. People know how to fight; they often don't know how to work through loss. Nor do they know how to live peacefully with those who disagree with them. Other people oppose any change at church since they believe church is, or certainly should be, a "change-free zone." This response may be a result of large stressors in other areas of their lives or they may have a deep aversion to examining their beliefs in any form. They believe their congregation should be a peace-filled, safe place.

Additionally, depending on how your congregation thinks about its mission and how it relates to the larger society, some members, or entire congregations, may resist any efforts to adapt to social changes. For example, should more contemporary music be used, should women be allowed more expanded roles, or should we welcome those unlike us? Rather than adapting to their changing neighborhoods and society members believe that new people need to change to fit the current congregation, since it's worked for so long. In fact, I once attended a congregation where a long-time member told me explicitly, "If you're not like us you won't be here long." He was not referring to theology but to social practices within the congregation. Although I didn't believe him at the time, in the end he was right.

Conflict is common in congregations without factoring in change. In stressed or unhealthy congregations conflict can be a way of life. Even within healthy, prospering congregations, conflict is common. Indeed, Peter Steinke, an expert on working with conflict in congregations argues that neither Church history nor Christian theology support a conflict-free environment.[21] Thus, our goal is not to extinguish conflict but to work with it constructively.

This chapter offers some perspectives on working with conflict during change. Entire books have been written for pastors and staff about working with conflict and this chapter is not meant to replace those texts. Rather, this chapter offers laity and pastors some ways of thinking about how to work with conflict, especially conflict generated by change initiatives.

Resistance 101

As I noted in the chapter on adaptive challenges, significant change is difficult work indeed. It's threatening, uncomfortable, and time-consuming and it takes personal and congregational energy. So it's no surprise that individuals and groups resist change initially. However, resistance has many faces and wise change agents learn to recognize them.

Donna Markham has explored the various roles resistance plays within congregations.[22] She claims that sometimes resistance is healthy for the community and will actually support change later on. The goal of all resistance is to make one feel safer, not necessarily to thwart change. When people feel unsafe they resist and one way of making them feel unsafe is to rush people into a decision they haven't owned. A constructive way of working with resistance is to develop a patient stance toward implementing the change. Here's why.

As leaders and change agents consider potential changes, they have taken their time. Often they will consider a new direction for a year or more. They are able to modulate their own anxiety on the issues. They can lay the issue aside for a time, spending time on it later, and think about it from differing angles. At the end of this process they are convinced of their direction and present their new idea to the congregation. What they then expect to happen is that the community will embrace the new direction and immediately begin to move forward.

What they forget is that the community will need at least as long, and probably longer, to own the change before they start to move. Individual members need time to own the proposed change for themselves. The majority of the group won't move until it has owned the change. This reality means the leader will be talking about the change for the next *year,* not the next month or two. Leaders often find this time incredibly frustrating. Why can't people see and own what is obviously so clear and so right? The resistance to the new direction that arises here allows people time to accommodate new ideas. Indeed, those who immediately embrace the idea have probably been thinking along the same lines for a year as well. Resistance and its associated conflict give the group time to acclimate. Pushing over or through this healthy resistance will worsen conflict and make the proposed change more difficult to implement. Understanding this pattern is especially important in congregations. Since congregations are voluntary associations (see Chapter 2), people don't have to comply with the leadership or policies as they do at work. They can choose to resist in a variety of ways, mostly without repercussion. Fostering change in a voluntary situation is very different from driving it in a market-based business.

However, Markham notes that resistance is not always healthy. Unhealthy resistance can be clothed with a surface peace. She labeled this resistance static resistance. The goal of static resistance is to thwart change and maintain the status quo. It's evidenced by poor communication, hidden agendas, secrets, and a pressure toward uniformity. Indeed, the peace that everyone so longs for can actually be an indicator of disease rather than health. If your congregation has a pattern of static resistance to change, it will be more difficult for the community to adopt change at all. Indeed, addressing static resistance is an adaptive challenge in itself.

Alternately, agitated resistance, which is an open response to change, while engendering a number of difficult behaviors, is actually a more healthy response. The key is in dealing constructively with the resistant behaviors. Those behaviors include denial, rigidity and control, thwarting collaboration, blaming, and so forth. Wise leaders, as they take time to let the group own the change can also frame these behaviors for the group publicly and without blame. Objectivity toward the resistance is important as is exploring members' understanding of why the resistance is occurring and what the implications of the behaviors might be. Rather than being publicly frustrated by resistant behaviors, it can be more helpful to portray them as part of the process of moving forward and work with people as they begin to adapt. However, some congregations will have more difficulty with conflict and change than others.

A Common Bond or a Common Identity?

As noted in Chapter 5, how a congregation is formed will have an effect on how it weathers conflict. Congregations can either be formed as a common identity or a common bond group.[23] Common identity congregations begin as a group of people with a common vision or mission. People may initially not know each other well but join because they resonate with the vision. Members are committed to achieving the mission and relationships revolve primarily around a shared commitment. When this vision is healthy, the congregation will grow and enter into mission. Yes, deep relationships do develop over time, but the center of the group is the shared mission. These common identity congregations withstand conflict better and are more stable in the face of change. They tend to be overall healthier as a group.

Common bond congregations were initially founded by a group of friends who wanted to worship together. The relationships, rather than the mission, are primary. Common bond congregations depend on everyone knowing and liking each other. It's important that everyone have very similar attributes and beliefs. These congregations withstand conflict poorly since the true goal is for everyone to be happy together. When interpersonal harmony disappears in the face of conflict, the community blows apart. Additionally, these congregations will have a difficult time welcoming new members or accommodating difference in themselves or others. They will exclude those who are different or threaten this harmony, even if they are leaders or long-term members who have come to believe differently about particular issues. Sometimes a common bond group will convert to a common identity group in the face of an outside threat. Unfortunately, fear, while very effective at unifying a group around an issue, is to be used with caution since it doesn't lead to health over time.

If you wish to work constructively with conflict in your congregation understanding its founding story is crucial. If you are in a common bond congregation, change will be more difficult and the ensuing conflict deeper and more damaging. One of the reasons for this reality is that the conflict will manifest as relational conflict rather than task conflict.

Task and Relational Conflict

Many people think that any type of conflict, particularly in a congregation, is bad. They work hard to keep peace, often at any cost. However, some types of conflict are actually good for the health of the community, while others are not.

Task conflict is conflict over what to do and how to do it, hence the reference to *task*. For example, task conflict may involve how to balance the budget, improve a program, or develop a policy. Some amount of task conflict actually improves the congregation's health and functioning as long as it doesn't get out of hand. It causes members to more deeply examine their decisions, suggest more options, and leads to improved implementation of ideas. Task conflict also protects against groupthink, which I'll talk about in a later chapter. Thus, if you want good decisions, good decision implementation, and higher functioning out of your congregation, you should actually encourage some task conflict in council and committee meetings. This approach can be achieved by council and committee leaders actively seeking a wide variety of ideas and encouraging deep examination of these ideas. Meetings need to be safe places for members to disagree as well as safe places to openly discuss existing conflicts.

Relational conflict, on the other hand, is to be actively controlled. Relational conflict involves actions like blaming, name-calling, assassinating character, and maximizing style/personality differences. It sometimes consists of small repeated jabs at someone or consistently negative body language, such as eye-rolling, directed at another. The goal is not to solve the problem at hand but to put the other person at a disadvantage through ridicule or accusation. Relational conflict leads to poor decision-making and poor functioning overall. No one feels safe so no one challenges what's going on.

The challenge is that some people are very adept at turning almost any task conflict, even minor ones, into full-blown relational conflict. These relational conflicts can then propagate throughout the congregation. For example, I was once a member of a board where an individual turned a simple decision about the group's meeting time into a relational conflict! Let me give another illustration. I attended a congregational meeting where the budget was being discussed. The treasurer was open about his process and figures but there were many questions since the congregation was in decline and the budget was very tight. People were concerned and trying to get a clear picture. Everything had been respectful and task-focused until the treasurer's wife stood up and accused the group of badgering her husband and of treating him badly. All talk of the budget ceased at that point. She had moved the discussion into relational conflict and no one felt safe to continue. Perhaps you have been in a similar meeting.

Relational conflict, especially in a congregation, can be deadly. It's extremely effective at thwarting change since it increases the perceived interpersonal threat level. Yet it's very common and some people are quite skilled at using it to protect themselves from change and loss. Very few of us do well with interpersonal threats. But there are ways of managing relational conflict.

Training your council and committee members in the concept of task conflict and relational conflict is a place to start. Most people readily grasp the difference when it's explained. Then create a covenant with council and committee members that disallows relational conflict during meetings. If the relational conflict is mild, or is just a misstep on someone's part, refocus the group on the task at hand. When you refocus, you deliberately ignore the relational affront and return to task language by asking others how they would *solve* or *address* the problem. If someone persists in relational conflict the committee chair should stop the meeting, name the behavior, and review the covenant. Alternately, you can name the relational conflict, stop the meeting for a two-minute timeout of silence, and then restart, refocused on task conflict. If the relational conflict continues after this point, end the meeting and address relational issues at another time. Let's look at a sample dialogue to explore how the process works.

Chair:	Some people want another type of worship service. Is it a good idea?
Lisa:	I think we do need another type of service. I would like a contemplative service in the evening. I think many people would come.
John:	I think that's a bad idea.
Chair:	Tell me more about that.
John:	Our morning service is fine. Anyone who wants something different is divisive.
Chair:	I understand that you feel uncomfortable with Lisa's idea. What do the rest of you think about offering a contemplative service?
John:	I said I thought it was a bad idea. Anyone who would go is crazy! Lisa always has these stupid ideas!
Chair:	John, we had agreed as a group to treat each other with respect. Your comments are not respectful. What do the rest of you think about Lisa's idea?

Frank: I like Lisa's idea and would like to send out a survey
           to see if others are interested.

In this dialogue, note how the chair did not let John turn the meeting into a relational conflict between John and Lisa. He kept the rest of the group involved and called John on his behavior. If John had persisted in trying to generate relational conflict, the chair would have ended the meeting and talked with John separately, requiring that he honor the group's covenant to remain on the committee.

Most of us feel uncomfortable with group conflict and avoid it. This avoidance is a major reason why many gifted people don't serve on congregational committees. They've had bad experiences in the past, especially with relational conflict. Yet task conflict, handled well, enables the group to move forward creatively. The same is true for agitated resistance in the face of change. Understanding resistance and conflict is central to wisely enacting change.

The take away

➢ Significant change will generate conflict. The key is working with it constructively.
➢ Resistance can be healthy since it gives people time to own the new idea.
➢ Your congregation's founding story will affect how it adapts to change.
➢ Keeping all conflict as task conflict rather than relational conflict will foster health and growth.

Taking it further

➢ Can you identify resistance to change in your congregation? What does that resistance look like? What is the source of it?
➢ Are conflicts in your congregation primarily task conflict or relational conflict? How are significant conflicts usually managed?
➢ What happens in your congregation when relational conflict arises?
➢ How could you work to move (or keep) existing conflict as task conflict?

8

DISSENT IS NOT A DIRTY WORD

If you are working for change, acting as a change agent, you may also be acting as a dissident. Dissent often has a political connotation since that's where we most often hear the word used. Yet dissidents don't just live in oppressive foreign regimes. Nor are they only political agitators in the US. You meet dissidents at work, at school, and in your congregation. Pastors may be dissidents in their denomination. Change and dissent are very closely linked.

Dissent has many faces, some of which are familiar and some less so. Whistle-blowing is the most extreme form of dissent and probably the most well-known, but is uncommon in congregations unless there are illegal or immoral activities occurring. Whistle-blowing is hard on everyone involved and is really a final effort to get a significant wrong addressed. But dissent also involves boat-rocking, openly questioning the status quo, and often a focused effort for positive change.

Unfortunately, dissent, especially in congregations, is frequently a dirty word. It's used as a synonym for divisiveness, obstruction, and relational conflict, all of which should be viewed very negatively. Dissidents often have a hard life within congregations and in denominations. Yet without dissidents, much constructive change wouldn't occur. Thus, understanding what dissent is and how to act wisely as a dissident is vital when enacting change.

This chapter explores what dissent is, what its benefits actually are, some common misconceptions, and ways for dissidents and leaders to work together to foster constructive change.

Understanding Dissent

The goal of dissent is to change values and practices within a group. Dissent is not practiced by leaders toward the group. When leaders work to change values and practices, it's called leadership. Thus, if you're a leader, you're not a dissident, at least when referring to the group you're leading. As a pastor, you may be dissenting toward your denominational leaders, but not toward your congregation since you're leading it.

Dissidents may be group members or outside of the official leadership structure. To illustrate, a board may have a member who disagrees with the board's direction but chooses to remain on the board as the loyal opposition. Alternately, a congregational member may actively oppose the board's direction. Both are practicing dissent, just from different locations. Because dissidents are by definition not leaders, they are said to be working from below, since they function at the lower ends of the power structure. They have less power, less authority, and less voice than official leaders to achieve their goals. For example, a dissident may be a committee member trying to change the direction the committee is headed. The dissenting member doesn't set the committee agenda, control the dynamics of the meeting, or interface with other leaders. He or she has less control over what happens in the committee.

Dissent is not the same as complaining. Most congregations have habitual complainers who complain about nearly everything. It's too hot, the children are too noisy, the sermon was boring, the music was dull, the carpet is dirty, and someone (not them) should do something. Dissent is different than complaining because it is focused on achieving a specific change in values and/or practices. It goes against the dominant view rather than supporting the status quo. Dissent is active and when you hand an issue to a dissident who cares about it, she or he works to address it.

However, dissent and complaining do share a link. During change people talk amongst themselves, which is fine up to a point. This airing of worry, concern, and disagreement with a proposed direction among friends is sometimes called lateral dissent.[24] In lateral dissent you want to find out if you're the only one with a problem. You want to find out if others agree. You mull over the issue as a group of acquaintances and refine its description. This initial lateral dissent can form the foundation for active dissent as people begin to understand and own their position on the topic. But lateral dissent, by itself, is ineffective for change because it's passive. It ends with, "yeah, we have a problem here" or "wouldn't it nice someday to . . ." or a continual, low-level griping but no one will step up and take some risk. No one will act. Parking lot meetings are most commonly lateral dissent. They're good up to a point and pointless thereafter.

Dissent is actually a positive action because it's pro-social, which means that dissidents are trying to accomplish what they believe to be beneficial change for the group. Dissidents believe that if their change was to occur, the congregation, as a whole, would benefit. It would grow, or more people would serve, or there would be an increase in enthusiasm or commitment. If leaders examine dissent from the dissidents' viewpoint, the benefits become obvious. That doesn't mean that leaders are going to agree with the proposed benefits or the path to get there. It does mean, though, that the dissident's overall goal is to benefit the group. Dissidents are not trying to destroy the congregation, although they are commonly accused of doing so. In reality, dissent is actually a type of loyalty toward the congregation. Dissidents, at great social risk to themselves, are trying to enact a change that's important. By choosing to speak out and act, they are demonstrating that the congregation, the mission, and/or the beliefs are important enough to take the risks that dissent entails.

To take this positive approach to dissent even further, dissent in a group is also always true, in some part. It's not usually completely true, but it is at least partially true. For example, are some people being excluded, is the group not living its mission, or are marginal voices being silenced? Is there an elephant in the room? These are areas where dissent is common. Dissidents are pointing out a legitimate issue, but perhaps they don't know all the factors or their proposed solution won't work. Yet there is always a kernel of truth in what they say and want. Dissidents are not crazy crackpots. Instead, they are seeing something the congregation is ignoring and perhaps wants to continue to ignore.

Dissent also tends to be focused on change regarding a specific issue or topic, rather than on changing everything. If dissidents were focused on changing everything, they wouldn't be able to exist within the community for long since the psychological and social pressures would be too high. They tend to put a high price on "walking the talk" regarding their specific issue. For example, dissidents might work to expand the role of women or increase social justice efforts, but they may be fine with the worship service and the education program. Or, the opposite may be true.

Unfortunately, I often find that leaders confuse dissent with obstruction, equating dissent with resistance to change rather than generating change. Yet dissent and obstruction function quite differently. True dissent is primarily task-focused and skilled dissidents keep the focus on their issue. They work to change what we do or how we think and avoid relational conflict, at least publicly. Dissent is also focused on a specific issue or a related set of issues. Obstruction, on the other hand, is not pro-social since it is not concerned with expanding benefits to the group. It tends to not be focused on a specific issue, but attacks a wide range of topics. It also tends to be personality-focused with an "I'm not going to let them do anything" attitude. Thus, obstruction is largely negative, where dissent can be a positive force and has many benefits, even if the change doesn't occur as the dissident exactly envisioned.

Benefits of Dissent

Dissent has many positive benefits for the congregation when it's handled well. First, dissent lessens groupthink, which is the bane of small group decision-making (more on this in Chapter 10). Church councils, committees, and sometimes even entire congregations routinely practice groupthink, which is an inability to consider all of the parts of a problem and all of the potential solutions. The group is working with blinders on and pursues a foolish direction as a result. Dissent seems to liberate creative and divergent thinking among group members. It fosters innovative thinking and supports change. Research shows that dissent, even when factually wrong, reduces the pressure on others in the group to conform. It seems to open a door to thinking outside the box. Dissent will cause other group members to consider multiple perspectives and new alternatives. Thus, groups with even one dissenter make better decisions.[25]

Sometimes dissent is called minority influence, since dissidents are in the minority. When there are minority views expressed, research shows that people tend to think more carefully about what is being argued. Most people come to decision-making with a good will and really want to make a good decision. The presence of a minority view makes them think overall about possible options. Even if they decide not to adopt the minority view, it has opened them up in many ways to thinking differently than before.[26]

The key is to keep dissent focused on the issue, so it's task conflict. Task conflict generates better understanding between people. When there is no conflict, people think they understand each other, but often don't since there is little actual conversation about values and practices. People assume everyone agrees with them.[27]

Dissent can be a positive force, especially when a congregation needs to engage in change. It enables people to think more openly and creatively. It surfaces issues that need to be addressed. Yet in spite of these benefits, especially during our current high level of social and economic change, dissent is strongly devalued, both by leaders and by other members who want to keep the peace. Unfortunately, a misreading of the Bible is often used to silence dissidents.

Dissent in the Bible

One of the difficulties with enacting dissent in a congregation is that leaders and the community as a whole use the Bible to shut down dissent by emphasizing the need for peace and unity. Yet Peter Steinke asserts that in the Bible justice is more important than tranquility.[28] Thus, we need to take a closer look at what the Bible says about dissent and conflict as well as peace.

In the Old Testament (Hebrew Scriptures), the prophets are the most obvious example of dissent. We admire those prophets who stood against the foes of Israel. We talk about their courage and their obedience to God. They're portrayed as heroes. What we don't talk about is how much of the prophets' dissent was directed inward. Sometimes it was to wealthy hypocrites, as in Amos' attack on the cows of Bashan (Amos 4). Other times it targeted the religious rulers (see Ezekiel 34). These prophets fit the definition of dissent since they were pro-social and calling for reform.

In the New Testament (Christian Scriptures) we also see dissent. Some argue that one of Jesus' goals was to reform *halakah*, the Jewish ethical law. You can see this goal at work when you read, "You have heard it said . . . but I say to you. . . ." Jesus healed on the Sabbath (see Matthew 12: 9-14) and emphasized knowing and obeying God over traditions of purity and power (see Mark 7: 1-13). Further, it is impossible to miss that Jesus is consistently disagreeing with religious authorities and even openly provoking them.

In the epistles we see a mixed picture. In Romans 13, Paul admonishes us to obey our secular leaders. This theme shows up in other places as well, asking us to obey our religious leaders. Yet there is another theme of obeying God, not people (see Acts 5:29), of disobeying authorities when they oppose God's path. There are arguments between Peter and Paul, (Galatians 2), Paul and John Mark and Barnabas (Acts 15:39), as well as continual theological debate. Indeed, Steinke notes that early Christianity was filled with conflict.[29]

Many like to portray the Church as peaceful, but this is not what the text or history says. Christian history is littered with dissent. Early martyrs, medieval mystics, and scores of reformers have all practiced some form of dissent. Most Protestant denominations arose from active dissent. Here again, as with the Hebrew prophets, we have developed only part of the story. We portray reformers as heroes, but downplay that their dissent was turned inward toward the Church. Thus, we use a dissident history to uphold the status quo and silence current dissent equally focused on reform.

Others believe that uniformity in outlook and opinion is evidence of God's leading. Thus, obeying Scripture (or God) means that everyone should believe exactly the same about a topic. In contrast, the Christian Scriptures support a stance of pursuing unity over uniformity. In unity we may disagree about some topics, but agree to honor God and each other in that disagreement. I Corinthians 12 explores the diverse abilities and perspectives that members may bring to a congregation, asking that this diversity be viewed as a gift. Uniformity is not the path to unity and peace, but is instead a counterfeit of unity. Unity is a work of the Holy Spirit, something we protect and work on through dialogue, prayer, and love. Sometimes dissent is the only path toward unity in the end. It is unity that is a mark of holiness, not uniformity.

Reaping the Benefits of Dissent as a Leader

Dissent goes against the dominant view. When a congregation is in decline and needs to change or is seeking a new path in some area, supporting and protecting dissent is a good place to start. Bringing dissidents to the table, listening, and understanding their views can open doors to new ways of thinking. Here are some ideas for supporting pro-social dissent.

Wise leaders develop a specific discipline of listening to dissent. I use the word discipline deliberately since it is always easier for leaders to listen to those who agree with them and with the dominant view. Dissidents should be sought out, rather than shunned. Wise leaders recognize that there is always some kernel of truth in dissent and they work to understand that truth. This kernel of truth also gives room for negotiation.

Second, wise leaders realize the need for negotiation. Once leaders have recognized what the issues actually are and where truth really is, they'll have opportunities to negotiate an authentic path forward. Change is a step-by-step process and every step may have multiple areas to negotiate solutions.

Third, wise leaders work to tell the truth about all of dissent in the Bible and Christian history. Telling the truth about dissent means talking about all of dissent, not just that focused outward. It means honoring dissidents' courage and obedience even when we don't like what they say. It means listening, honestly, to their voices because maybe we need to hear what they're saying even if we don't like it.

Fourth, wise leaders make room for dissidents at the idea table and decision-making table. Dissidents often represent those at the margins and those who are ignored or simply outvoted. These are the very people the congregation should want to draw in, yet all too often they are pushed out the door because their needs and beliefs may be a little different. If your congregation needs some good ideas, asking dissidents and those at the margins is a wise approach.

Finally, wise leaders become adept at managing conflict and decision-making. By becoming skilled at allowing and honoring divergent views they enable dissidents to be heard.

Practicing Dissent Wisely

Change agents also need to be wise in how they practice dissent in order to be effective. Here are some ideas.[30]

Change agents need to have a clear vision of what they want to achieve. This vision may involve many steps and significant time and energy. Thus, understanding the possible path(s) toward their goals is vital. Additionally, they need to be able to clearly articulate this vision to others. For example, saying "women should be allowed to do more" is not specific, which makes it hard for others to act on. Saying, "women should be allowed to participate in all decision-making" or "women should be allowed to be elders" is very specific.

Second, change agents need to be flexible when responding to others' views since inflexible dissidents are viewed as extreme, whether they actually are or not. They need to be open to negotiate for small wins and understand what possible options negotiation opens up. Since change is a multi-step process there are many possible paths forward. It's easy for dissidents to confuse highlighting an issue with everyone agreeing with their solution. They need to remember that while the issue is most likely legitimate their proposed solution may not be the best path forward.

Third, change agents need to work hard to involve others in the change process. Sometimes change agents can be comfortable being alone as they push for change. It seems easier and faster on the surface since negotiating with possible allies and bringing others on board consumes time and energy. But building alliances is an important strategy to pursue.

Finally, change agents should be very careful to keep their work issue-focused. As noted above and in Chapter 6, task conflict is effective in generating change. Relational conflict is not. As soon as your dissent veers into a relational realm, your opportunity for success dwindles drastically. Further, it can foment congregation-wide relational conflict, which is always destructive.

The take away

➤ Dissent is the basis for many congregational changes.
➤ Dissent, when practiced well, has many benefits for the congregation.
➤ The Bible actually supports some types of dissent.
➤ Congregations and change agents must work together to create a constructive environment for dissent.

Taking it further

➤ How does your congregation view those who disagree with the status quo?
➤ How is dissent currently occurring in your congregation? What issues are important?

➤ How can you create a constructive environment for dissent?
➤ As a change agent, what challenges do you face as you enact dissent?

9

WORKING WITH LOSS AND GRIEF

Americans are not good with grief. We no longer have many of the rituals of the past to create space for grieving. Our goal appears to be to get over it quickly and move on, even if it's grieving something truly significant like the death of a spouse or a child. We become frustrated with those who, for whatever reason, are unable to move on, especially on our timetable. We don't talk much about mourning, even with those obviously enmeshed in grief. We ignore the impact loss and grief have on us all.

Yet loss and grief are all around us. We experience a host of smaller losses during our lives. Many of these seemingly smaller losses can have life-altering consequences as well. A child starts school or goes to college. We change jobs or retire. We move to a new neighborhood or a new city. Friends move and relationships change. Each of these life changes involves grief because we lose something we value. Our way of life changes, our relationships change, as does our identity. Even when those changes are welcomed, there is always an associated loss. Sometimes the loss is outweighed by the positive aspects of change. We have a momentary feeling of loss and quickly move forward. Other times, seemingly welcome change generates a deep grief and we are caught off guard. We can't seem to move forward and embrace our new path.

If we reflect upon our lives we can see how loss and grief have played a part in creating who we are. However, we may not realize that loss and grief also play a part in the organizations in which we participate. At work, lay-offs, transfers, and even retirements generate grief because relationships and ways of being are disrupted for those who remain. Congregations are not grief-free either. While we think of our congregations as safe places to bring grief generated elsewhere, in reality congregations have their own losses. The sources of these losses are varied but many are associated with change. This chapter explores the role of loss and grief in congregational change and offers constructive ways of working with it.

Sources of Loss

As we've talked about in previous chapters, all change generates some loss. Adaptive challenges, in particular, generate strong feelings of loss since personal and organizational identities are shifting. As these identities shift and reorient to new and different ways of being, everyone stands to lose something. For those who welcome a change, the benefits can far outweigh any losses they'll experience. For other people, however, the losses loom far larger than any possible benefit.

Perhaps someone contributed an expertise that is no longer needed. He or she may have kept the grounds and now it's been handed off to a lawn service. Perhaps one's position of prestige is no longer available. She or he may have been the Sunday School superintendent, but now Sunday School has been reconfigured to an afterschool program for neighborhood children. Perhaps a person held significant power and in the new congregational structure that power is less. Perhaps relationships are affected. It's harder for friends to meet or cherished fellowship opportunities no longer occur. People may believe their well-being is affected somehow. Important events may be harder for them to attend or physical barriers, like driving at night, are suddenly present.

Many people are tempted to portray these losses as resistance and anger at the proposed change and ignore the underlying loss and its associated grief. It's easier and more socially acceptable to be angry than to grieve. However, anger doesn't address the actual issue. Surfacing the loss surrounding the proposed changed is important in moving forward.

One major source of loss is that some people feel they will lose God as a result of a proposed change.[31] While we would all agree theologically that losing God is impossible, losing a felt connection with God is, for some, a distinct possibility. Some congregational members have not nourished an attachment to God apart from the weekly worship space or service content. How the sanctuary appears, the order of service, and the music are the only way they connect with

God. In essence, they have turned God and church into the same entity. Thus, any change in seating or other aspects of the physical space, modifying the order of service, or changing the music generates a very strong response in these people. While it's true that these changes affect everyone in the congregation and the entire congregation may feel uneasy about the proposed change, some members will not be able to accommodate any significant (or sometimes even minor) change in the worship space or service content.

One of the reasons they are so inflexible is that the physical space and service content actually represent God to them and they can't conceive of meaningfully knowing God in any other fashion. The issue moves far beyond individual preferences or accommodating others into an issue of spiritual, as well as identity, survival. Additionally, since we often talk about how God is unchanging, it's a very short jump for them to believe that the congregation, and most especially worship, should be unchanging as well. From their viewpoint, losing God because of the proposed changes is going to happen and their resistance will be fierce, as perhaps it should be, when understood from their perspective.

Another source of loss is congregational decline. People like to think that their congregation will go on forever and they simply can't (or won't) believe that the congregation could be at the end of its lifecycle. This belief makes it doubly difficult to manage the losses suffered during decline. During decline the congregation slowly (and sometimes not so slowly) loses everything of importance. Cherished members are no longer able to attend or have died. Other members have left for healthier congregations. Activities such as Sunday School or even the women's group cease due to a lack of ability or interest. Ministry dwindles until only the worship service occurs and sometimes that's a struggle. Congregational meaning and identity erode as ministry dwindles. Everyone is living with ongoing, persistent, and long-standing grief. Unlike the loss and grief associated with adaptive challenges, which while it can be strong, is short-lived, the loss and grief arising out of decline is debilitating and ongoing. This persistent grief can set the stage for the congregation moving into an inconsolable state.

Inconsolability

Howard Stein has been studying grief in organizations for several decades and has claimed that organizations, like individuals, can become inconsolable.[32] Inconsolable organizations occur when the group experiences repeated traumas or losses, which they are officially not permitted to mourn. For example, a business may experience repeated, deep layoffs without any opportunity for those remaining to say goodbye to those leaving or to mourn the loss of dignity and meaning. Stein notes those who have left (or been laid-off) become invisible and mentioning them at work becomes taboo. Grief over lost relationships, lost dreams, and lost dignity can be forbidden by coworkers, supervisors, and executives. Eventually, one forbids oneself to grieve. The result is employees who are emotionally dead. The group becomes so engulfed in grief and loss that efforts to move the group forward, either from below or above, are futile. Motivation plummets.

Some of you in congregations in steep decline probably recognize Stein's concept of inconsolability. Congregations in decline suffer repeated losses. Long-time members die or can no longer attend. Others leave. Programs and ministries close down. The present is jeopardized and there is deep worry about the future. While it's easy to see the impact of these losses on people, few will talk about their grief openly. Rather than publicly mourning these losses in healthy ways, expressing grief becomes forbidden since people feel it portrays a lack of faith in God. True faith is portrayed as being upbeat. Instead, the congregation, and often the leaders as well, focus on how the next leader or God will deliver them and they will once again become successful. Thus, congregations become perfectly set up for becoming inconsolable.

To make matters worse, Stein also notes that Midwestern Whites struggle with expressing grief.[33] Their cultural values of indirect communication, face-saving, conflict avoidance, and peace at all costs make it difficult to grieve, especially in a group. It's considered shameful to let others know you have problems and persistent loss in a congregation is indeed a large problem. Thus, trying to effectively manage grief in a declining congregation in the Midwest or with Midwest roots or narratives can be particularly challenging.

Stein offers some suggestions for addressing inconsolability. First, it's important to recognize that working through grief, especially inconsolable grief, takes a long time. In a steeply declining congregation, it may take more time than you realistically have. Yet not working through it means the group is unable to do the necessary planning for whatever the future brings. Second, formal and informal leaders need to openly discuss the need to grieve over these persistent losses. Rather than glossing over loss while trying to push people forward, leaders need to become the chief mourner and encourage others to enter into this space of mourning. Storytelling can give voice to grief and begin the process of mourning. In contrast, motivational strategies often impair grieving since they dismiss the importance of the losses. These losses are especially significant during decline.

Working with Grief in Decline

Like Stein, Harrison Owen[34] has researched how organizations work with grief. As with Stein, his research has been based in business, but much of it applies to congregations in decline as well.

As noted above, some people in the congregation refuse to believe that the congregation's life is coming to an end. Their commitment to the congregation, which was once such a source of strength to them and to the group as a whole, now becomes a source of despair. Unfortunately, this pattern is most common is some of the most committed lay leaders. Thus, talking about steep decline with these lay leaders can be challenging. They may be the most resistant to considering realistic alternatives and the angriest toward the pastor and denominational executives.

Just as people like to believe that congregations live forever, they also like to think that any leader who was in charge at the end has somehow caused the death. As noted in Chapter 5, decline is usually a decades-long process that people only notice as it becomes severe. The belief that leaders are at fault makes the work of the pastor and engaged laity truly difficult. During decline the role of leaders is to lead during the life cycle, not thwart it. Leading at the end means entering into grief-work and helping members decide if they should move toward renewal or resurrection to decide to close.

In renewal or resurrection a congregation as it is currently constructed can end and have its spirit or its mission continue on in a new and different work. Sometimes the congregation completely closes for awhile, planning to reopen with a different focus later. Other times a small remnant moves forward. In any case, the original congregation dies and the mission continues with a largely new group, a differently constructed group.

Effective grief-work is what makes renewal or resurrection possible. Part of effective grief-work is moving through the stages of transition listed below. The point of grief-work is to help everyone let go of the existing structure so that they can begin to envision alternatives. In the case of decline those alternatives may mean closing the congregation and helping individuals move on in a positive fashion.

Owen lists three stages of grief-work. Those of you familiar with how grief can be exhibited in individuals may recognize a similar pattern for a congregation. First, there's shock and anger that congregational death is indeed very possible. This realization can result in major pyrotechnics in the group. As the open anger dies away, members move into denial and use many "if only" statements. Initially, this process provides some space for the new reality to sink in and members must be given time to accommodate to it. However, if this time is extended and members refuse to move forward, the end result is congregational death, not renewal.

The retelling of stories and memories can set the stage for renewal. With skillful guidance this stage can transform into imagining a new future for the congregation, one where the original mission persists even if the original members don't. However, if the members remain rooted in the past, renewal won't occur. The move from memory to imagination is hard to see, since the words are the same, but the feeling is very different. Once the group is in the realm of imagination, renewal is possible. This storytelling can also support change not related to decline.

Moving through Change and Transitions

William Bridges has written extensively on organizational and personal transitions during change and I have adapted his thoughts to a congregational setting.[35] *Transition* is the time between recognizing the need for change and the change actually being enacted. Significant change takes time, usually far longer than anyone desires or anticipates. This in-between time is vital for moving forward in a healthy way. However, it's also deeply uncomfortable and people often opt out of the process because of the discomfort. Instead, they implement change as quickly as possible with poor results. Bridges claims transition has several stages, each with its challenges.

Bridges' first stage of transition is saying goodbye to the way life has been in the congregation. Saying goodbye well is important since a failure to have a good ending is a leading cause of failure in new projects. People can't effectively move forward while dragging the past with them. During the goodbye stage people begin disengaging from the way things are. Yet the congregation doesn't do this step all at the same time. Some people have been disengaged for a while since they couldn't live within the current reality. Others will find disengaging very slow and difficult since the current reality feeds their needs for relationships, prestige, power, and/or stability. These people will feel their losses most strongly.

As saying goodbye takes hold in the congregation, people begin to shift how they identify with the congregation. This process makes sense because congregational identity is shifting. Perhaps they strongly identified with the music, but now music is changing. Since their point of identity has changed, their relationship with the congregation shifts as well.

As the process of saying goodbye nears its end, people feel detached. They have trouble making sense of what's going on. This process makes sense because significant change means that the narratives we talked about in Chapter 4 need to be revised. Since narratives or stories are how we make sense of reality, then of course reality is hard to understand when the narratives shift. People no longer feel anchored.

Individually, people cycle through these stages as they accommodate change and loss. The stages are not hierarchical. Within a congregation you will see people in all of stages of goodbye at any one time. During the process of saying goodbye some people leave the congregation. They may leave because they don't agree with the direction, their identity points were few and now they're gone, or they're addressing other losses in their lives and can't manage yet another one. For some, the loss of the congregation seems less than what they would lose if they stayed.

Eventually, the majority of people have said goodbye and are ready to move forward. Yet what happens next doesn't feel much like moving forward, it feels like moving into a gray fog. Bridges calls this stage the neutral zone. Initially in the neutral zone people feel disoriented. The feeling of having left their former way of being really sinks in. People feel lost and don't know how to move forward. Goals don't motivate people and congregational energy and enthusiasm are low. Everyone seems to be waiting, but for what is unclear.

As this gray fog of waiting takes hold, old ways of being start to disintegrate. Old interpersonal conflicts, long buried, arise. It's hard to keep old rituals and structures together. Old issues, apparently resolved long ago, rear again. Grief often manifests as anger and that pattern can be most true here. It can really feel like the group is unraveling, but the key is to recognize that before a new way of being can be created, the old way must die. During this disintegration is another place where people sometimes leave. They were able to manage the grief of saying goodbye, but they are unable to accommodate this grayness, this winter, this emptiness of waiting for new life to emerge.

Eventually, this emptiness generates a space for new ideas and new ways of being. People discover new ways of being together and enacting ministry. As these new ways take hold, the longed-for change begins to emerge and grow. However, while I have talked about this process in an organic way, many people need to be explicitly taught how to act in the new reality. Interestingly, some people decide to leave at this point. They've persevered through the grief of saying goodbye as well as the gray time of waiting. They've made it through, but now they can't understand how to live with the fully embodied change. They can't adapt, so they leave.

Using Rituals during Change and Decline

One of the most helpful strategies for working with loss and grief is the use of rituals. Since surfacing loss and grief are vital to moving forward constructively, wise leaders become skilled at planning rituals that enable people to process their grief. Several types of rituals are possible.

One ritual could involve publicly releasing people from their call to serve in a particular ministry. For example, some congregations have a formal time of call or recognition for teachers, youth workers, and leaders at the beginning of their ministries. As ministries end, publicly thanking people for their service and blessing them creates a positive sense of closure, both for the individual and the congregation. It also supports clean handoffs of leadership.

Alternately, as a ministry ends, the congregation could institute a ritual of having a celebratory meal where past accomplishments and work are recognized and blessed. Again, this ritual creates a positive sense of closure and also enables extended times of storytelling that can serve as the foundation for moving forward. For example, if a long-standing Bible study or fellowship opportunity is ending, having a celebration creates a healthy path for closure.

Another way to surface grief is to create an entire service of mourning for losses. This strategy is more suited to congregations nearing closure or exploring how to move through deep decline. The lament Psalms can serve as a rich resource here. Again, focusing on extended storytelling is important. This service would function similar to a funeral wake.

As I've observed how congregations experience grief I'm always amazed at how poor Christians are at working with endings, loss, and grief. We have the resurrection story at our center and a God who is ever-present and ever-working in all things. Yet God is left out of the picture when we grieve at church. Allowing God to be in the midst of our losses is truly the only way to move forward.

The take away

➤ Loss and grief are an inherent part of any change process and certainly of congregational decline.
➤ During change, entering into transition time is important to moving forward well.
➤ Learning to manage grief during decline can make the difference between congregational renewal and death.

Taking it further

➤ If your congregation is involved in change, who stands to lose the most and why? How are they embodying their grief?
➤ Are congregational leaders talking about loss and grief? If so, how?
➤ If your congregation is in decline, how is loss embodied in your congregation?
➤ What strategies are your leaders using to constructively work with grief?
➤ What rituals would be useful in your congregation?

10

THE MANY PITFALLS OF DECISION-MAKING

The ability to make good decisions is one of the hallmarks of being a mature adult. Mature adults are able to master their impulsiveness, gather information, weigh the information, seek counsel from others if needed, and act in the best interest of themselves and others. Unfortunately, we all know adults of a mature age who are still unskilled at making good decisions. Their lives and the lives of those around them bear the results of these poor decisions.

Groups of people also make decisions. Successful groups have learned how to take in information and assess it, listen to their members, and develop a plan. However, since there are many individuals involved, group decision-making can be more challenging. It can be especially difficult if the group is undergoing significant change or feels threatened in some way.

Congregations seem to struggle more with good decision-making than other types of organizations. Leaders and members receive little explicit training in how make good decisions. Congregational attributes, which I'll explore below, predispose them to difficulties. Poor congregational decision-making results in being unable to manage change, congregational splits, ministries failing, and decline. Thus, implementing good decision-making practices is vital for congregational success. This chapter explores common decision-making pitfalls and offers strategies for avoiding them.

Cult-like Behavior

Most Christians associate the term *cult* with what they consider to be heretical beliefs about the nature of God, the nature of humans, salvation, and other very significant points of theology. However, cults also often have distinctive beliefs about authority and group decision-making. Thus, it's possible to have orthodox Christian theology but have cult-like behavior within a particular congregation. Indeed, some congregations, depending on how they think about leadership and authority, may be particularly prone to cult-like behavior.

Several hallmarks of cult-like behavior can appear within congregations. These hallmarks include a demand that everyone submit to formal leadership; a belief that congregational members are holy and right while other Christians are not; a devaluing of critical thinking about issues and decisions; a belief that fulfillment can only be achieved within the congregation; and severely sanctioning those who leave.[36] Many congregations may have mild aspects of these behaviors. However, when a congregation openly exhibits several of these behaviors simultaneously it can be a sign of cult-like dynamics.

When these behaviors are in place, it makes it very difficult for effective or healthy decision-making to occur. Dissent, or even questioning, is forbidden, as is open discussion of options or issues. As a result, the cult-like behavior becomes self-reinforcing and is very difficult to address by those inside. Fortunately, many of these groups tend to be unstable over time. Unfortunately, they can do great damage to individuals while they last.

Groupthink

Some of us have heard the phrase "all great minds think alike." Usually people use this phrase to signal they agree with others' ideas. However, when all great minds *do* think alike, the result is often groupthink. In groupthink the decision-makers are unable to gather all the appropriate information, assess risks and consequences appropriately, and make a good decision for the current situation. Congregations, by their very nature are more prone to groupthink than many other types of organizations.

Irving Janis has spent much of his career studying how groups of smart people can make such bad decisions.[37] Based on his examination of high-profile decisions he claims there are several underlying conditions in groups that suffered groupthink. Unfortunately, these conditions describe many congregations.

Many congregational councils, and often congregations as well, are quite homogenous. That is, they share similar beliefs (required for membership), life experiences, and ethnic and socioeconomic backgrounds. This homogeneity means that it's much easier for great minds to think alike. Similarly, many congregations are fairly cohesive and boards are even more so. Homogenous, highly cohesive groups will easily drift toward groupthink since there is little pressure to consider alternative ideas. Indeed, it's hard in this situation not to enter into it.

Second, whether the congregation believes in consensus decision-making or not (and some groups, such as the Society of Friends (Quakers), explicitly practice consensus decision-making), many congregations informally believe that a strong consensus is required. This consensus is often understood as God's direction since if the group prays for guidance, even in a marginal way, God will lead everyone in the same direction. Indeed, few congregations will call a pastor or move forward with a major decision without a very high level of agreement. This pressure toward consensus, while not bad in itself, makes it more difficult for people to offer alternative ideas or to thwart groupthink when it occurs. It becomes easy to portray a dissenter as "not listening to God." However, as noted in Chapter 7, the Christian story is full of conflict and differing views among believers.

Sometimes councils are isolated and insulated from congregational feedback. Elders may be seen as anointed and thus not open to question. Or, the council may hold all of their meeting content as confidential. I once attended a congregation where the all-male board was not allowed to share any information outside the group, not even with their wives. This practice resulted in some interesting marital dynamics when one of the wives forcefully disagreed with a board decision during a public meeting!

Councils often have little instruction in effective decision-making, instead relying on personal practices, which are often lacking. Even those council members who engage in effective decision-making practices at work can feel they are inappropriate for church since they may not seem spiritual. Thus, council meetings can easily drift into all-out relational conflict or groupthink and miss effective practices. Further, many councils and congregations use Robert's Rules of Order, which is actually a process for the orderly conduct of meetings, not for ensuring a good decision. If a group is enmeshed in groupthink, Robert's Rules will support whatever decision it makes.

Councils often lack impartial leadership, which means that it can be difficult or unsafe to offer alternative ideas. Quality decision-making depends on a thorough survey of all appropriate options. Instead, leaders can come expecting or requiring a rubber stamp to their own favorite ideas rather than a frank discussion of options.

Finally, for those congregations in steep decline or other difficulty, groupthink is more of a risk.[38] The group can feel a strong external threat and believe they have a low chance of success. When the congregation feels under threat it's more likely to grasp at the (same) straw even though it's not a good idea. Additionally, groups under threat tend to be rigid and won't consider good alternatives as viable since they are perceived as too risky.[39] They will stay the course, even a bad course, rather than engage even a low level of risk that is unknown.

Groupthink Behaviors

Although Janis notes several behaviors in groups that engaged in groupthink, I want to highlight three that are most common in congregations. First, the decision-making group believes it is invulnerable and has a high view of its own morality. These beliefs result in excessive optimism and lead members to ignore ethical consequences. In short, the group believes they are too good, too careful, and too right to fail. Congregational councils can easily fall into this trap since it can be easy for them to believe that God is on their side and won't let them fail (even though they may not have actually consulted God).

A second behavior is to ignore and disparage those who disagree with the proposed action. As I explored in Chapter 8, dissent can lead to better decision-making by offering alternatives or by openly questioning a decision, thus allowing everyone to think more deeply about the issue. During groupthink it doesn't even take a seasoned dissident to question a decision. Almost anyone outside of the decision-making group can identify the potential for disaster. Yet the decision-makers accuse those who disagree of not being true believers, of not "catching God's vision for us," or of being troublemakers. They will not allow frank discussion of the decision or consider other alternatives.

A third behavior is a pressure toward uniformity. As I discussed in Chapter 8, uniformity is a counterfeit practice quite different from unity, which is the work of the Holy Spirit. This pressure toward uniformity can take several paths. It may occur as direct pressure against alternative views. Disagreeing can be so uncomfortable that people just won't do it. Similarly, group members can self-censor their doubts so that they can go along with the group. In short, while people will recognize a bad idea, they are unwilling to challenge it because of the social risk involved. Sometimes there is minimal discussion and the leader assumes quickly that the group agrees. He or she may open a discussion with saying, "Since I know we all agree, let's take a vote" thus making it difficult to squeeze in any objection and glossing over any potential disagreement. And, sometimes there are self-appointed guards who work to keep out any disconfirming evidence to the discussion since "it's not really important and would just muddy the issue." As a result, those who would speak up can't get their concerns in front of the group.

Effective Decision-making

Based on his research, Janis offers some criteria for effective decision-making. These criteria can be used to implement methods for sound council and congregational decisions. First, the group should gather all pertinent information regarding the issue. Whenever there has been an incomplete search for information or pertinent information is discounted without cause, groupthink is a distinct possibility.

Second, the group's objectives and its values need to be clearly understood. What is the group trying to achieve? What values relate? For example, why is the congregation starting a new ministry? How does this ministry explicitly relate to the congregation's call to enact the gospel in its setting? How does the proposed action uphold Christian or denominational values?

Third, the group needs to honestly map all the possible costs and consequences, positive and negative, of all proposed decisions. Costs and consequences extend beyond financial concerns. Who stands to lose what and why? How will ministry be affected? Since doing nothing is also a choice, the consequences of failing to decide should also be weighed. In particular, the costs and consequences of the most favored action should be examined closely. Members should continue to explore alternatives since this mapping of costs and consequences will often reveal new possibilities. Members need to seek advice from seasoned experts as needed and carefully weigh it, even if it negatively impacts their best choice. Note that Janis so far has emphasized the gathering and honest analysis of information. Groups engaged in groupthink latch onto one preferred idea and move rapidly forward, ignoring disconfirming information along the way. Thus, one way to protect against groupthink is to require a strong practice for gathering and analyzing information.

Finally, if the group has done its task well, it will have a clear understanding of the potential pitfalls of its chosen route. Wise groups construct realistic contingency plans for when these pitfalls arise. They are rarely caught completely off-guard since they have made some provisions ahead of time.

Groupthink is hard to dislodge once it has taken root. This difficulty is particularly true in congregations since they share so many underlying predispositions that reinforce it. The easiest ways to dislodge groupthink are actually to disband the group completely or to introduce a number of new members simultaneously so that the pattern is broken. Thus, preventing groupthink is far easier than fixing it after the fact.

Honoring dissent and viewing it as a constructive force is one way to prevent groupthink. Another is to create an atmosphere in meetings where all concerns can be aired and openly considered. Still another strategy is to consider the quality of leadership in the group. Sometimes strong leaders can inadvertently create groupthink by vigorously arguing for their direction so that others feel unable to disagree. Or, if there is a dearth of leadership, the group can meander into groupthink or an Abilene paradox.

Taking a Trip to Abilene

The Abilene paradox derives its name from a fictional story of a family taking a trip to Abilene, Kansas. The story recounts how the family is sitting on the farm on a hot, boring Sunday afternoon. Someone suggests the possibility of driving a couple hours to Abilene to get off the farm and eat dinner in town. Family members are not enthusiastic, but since they're hot, bored, and tired, they climb into the car and drive. As the story goes, when they return home everyone complains. The drive was hot and the scenery was boring. Abilene had little to recommend it and the dinner was lackluster. On top of everything they wasted money on gas. Family members are now complaining about going to Abilene.

What's interesting is that at the beginning of the trip the family knew how far it was to Abilene, what the scenery was like, what Abilene was like, what dinner would be like, and the price of gas. So, we have to ask, why did they go? Why did they do what they didn't really want to do to get a result they knew they would get? This situation of the group doing what it doesn't want to do is the Abilene paradox.

Jerry Harvey has termed the Abilene paradox the management of agreement.[40] Usually, in council meetings we worry about managing disagreement and conflict, especially relational conflict, and this concern is well-founded. However, we also need to be concerned about managing agreement, especially when that agreement is unenthusiastic or the group has a habit of just going along.

Harvey explained how the Abilene paradox works. For example, your congregation may be facing a challenge. Your council members agree, in private, about the nature of the challenge. Your council members, in private, also agree about what steps to take to address the challenge. Thus, you would expect the council meeting to offer productive ideas of how to address the challenge. Instead, council members fail to publicly state their private beliefs and strategies to each other in the meeting. When the topic comes up in the council meeting, they vote, as a group, to take an action that each individually, in private, disagrees with. They enact their decision, but reap the bad result they privately expected and then complain, "We knew this would happen!" This pattern can repeat several times within a group.

Everyone in the group contributes to the problem. The trip to Abilene could have been stopped by any family member saying, "I don't want to go. It's hot, boring, and no fun. I'll stay home." Similarly, any council member could say "I think this idea is poor and here's why," or "Here's what I really think we need to do." Instead, group members don't want to stand up and own their actual beliefs and so everyone unenthusiastically goes along with what's expected and enacts poor decisions.

Groupthink and the Abilene paradox are linked by being based in dysfunctional group dynamics, but they also differ. Groupthink is trying to manage *disagreement* by shutting out disconfirming information and shutting down dissent. The Abilene paradox is managing *agreement* by members refusing to be honest with each other about what they believe. Harvey believes people don't act because of anxiety. People fear what will happen if they speak up. In groups that fail to manage agreement there is high frustration, feelings of impotence, and blaming. This reality is unlike groupthink where everyone is cheerfully running off a cliff while bystanders wring their hands and shout warnings or leave in frustration. With the Abilene paradox the challenge is getting people to own what they actually believe and actually want to do and enabling them to do it. In groupthink the challenge is to get people to believe that what they want to do may actually be wrong.

In both situations, creating safe opportunities for disagreement and dissent are important strategies. Similarly, encouraging open discussion and being aware of group dynamics is important. Group leaders have a key role in creating a safe meeting environment and in encouraging everyone to be honest and own the decision-making. Leaders also need to become skilled at using different types of meeting processes.

The Many "D's" of Decision-making

The 3Rs of grade school: Reading, (w)riting, and (a)rithmetic are familiar to many of us. Similarly, there are 3D's of decision-making: Debate, discussion, and dialogue. We seem to use these terms interchangeably, but they have very different meanings and uses. Knowing how and when to use each process can result in more effective meetings and more thoughtful approaches to challenges.

I once heard a lay sermon that began with, "I want to take this time to dialogue with you about . . . ." The speaker held decision-making power on an issue and I disagreed with his direction. I was instantly interested in participating because I wanted to dialogue on those topics with him. Instead, the congregation had a 20 minute defense (yet another D) of the status quo and why it was good. Clearly, the layman and I had very different ideas about what dialogue meant! And, realistically, I could have been wiser since I know it's impossible to dialogue from the pulpit using a written script. Let's explore the D's a little further.

The first D is *debate*. Debate is focused on convincing the other party you're right. The goal is persuasion, moving the other to your position. It's an "I'm-right-and-you're-wrong" approach with a long history in Western philosophy. Many feminists and those from other cultures claim debate is a Western male way of communicating. It's competitive and excludes those unskilled or disinterested in argumentation. It also worsens existing conflict, rather than quelling it since there is always a winner and a loser. Yet debate has a strong background in some Christian circles, especially regarding evangelism. I once heard a pastor claim that a high school debate class was his best preparation for the pastorate.

The second D is *discussion*. Discussion is focused on getting an answer and getting the work done. Discussion is used for decisions (still another D). It should be open to everyone involved in the decision (although we all know cases where that's not true). Discussion is best for making simple decisions fairly rapidly and is usually supported by voting of some type. Robert's Rules of Order is an example of a discussion process. Discussion, when done well, is fairly neutral regarding conflict, primarily because it should work with decisions with low potential for conflict.

The third D is *dialogue*. Dialogue is focused on truly understanding someone else, with a hopeful goal of creating a new, shared meaning or direction. The roots of the word are *dia (through)* and *logos (meaning/word)*. Thus, dialogue results in meaning flowing through people.[41] Dialogue is reflective and moves more slowly than debate and discussion. In dialogue all interested parties have a voice and there is no right or wrong idea. People engage in active listening, are open and respectful to differing views, and have an active, positive curiosity about what others think. The goal is to find areas of shared values or beliefs, rather than working to convince the other party of your values. The stance during dialogue is not "us vs. them" but rather "we are learning together."

Dialogue is suited for complex situations and for creating identity. In dialogue one still holds on to one's beliefs but listens deeply to the other, seeking areas of converging meaning. It does not involve voting. It is the most helpful approach when trying to prevent or quell conflict since it welcomes all to the table and values their input. It is also the most helpful approach for working with adaptive challenges.

When a congregation is undergoing change the many D's rear their heads. Some people want to engage in debate, often as a form of resistance, obstruction, or grief manifesting as anger. Debate is rarely appropriate in congregations and certainly not during change since it silences people and worsens conflict. Discussion can be very useful for addressing technical or hybrid problems and for just getting the simple work of managing congregational business done. However, during change, the most productive D is dialogue.

Unfortunately, most people are unskilled at dialogue. Its slow pace and high degree of ambiguity makes many Americans uncomfortable.

It seems very unproductive since it just looks like talking and talking is not the same as action and what we want during change is action. Yet dialogue is the only tool that supports the deep thinking required as identities change and narratives shift. It is really the only effective way to walk with people through their loss or through the gray time of transition. During change, leadership should focus on creating time and space for dialogue, not discussion, and certainly not debate. Unfortunately, the opposite seems to occur, with debate becoming more strident, discussion (and the associated voting) used for complex, hot-button topics, and dialogue disappearing altogether.

A Note about Silence

Some congregations include in their corporate confession of sins the phrase "things done and left undone." This chapter has explored things said (and done), but not the unsaid. Whenever we talk about decision-making we also need to talk about silence. What's true about silence is that it says nothing. It is *silent*. Unfortunately, many people use others' silence to support their own direction, saying, "If they disagreed, they would speak up." However, all you can truthfully say about silence is that it is *silent*. Beware of anyone using silence to argue support for their viewpoint. Are people silent because they agree? We don't know. Are they silent because they don't care or because they're afraid to talk? Again we don't know. Silence is an invitation to dialogue. In reality, what silence says is nothing until you explore further. If you note that someone is consistently silent take time to find out what they're actually thinking. You may be surprised!

The take away

- ➢ Some congregations, while theologically orthodox, engage in cult-like decision-making processes.
- ➢ Congregations are prone to groupthink and other poor decision-making practices.
- ➢ Learning when and how to use debate, discussion, and dialogue is important during change.
- ➢ Silence only tells you that people aren't talking.

Taking it further

- ➢ Does your congregation have aspects of cult-like group processes?
- ➢ Have you encountered groupthink in your congregation? If so, how did it occur? What were the results?
- ➢ Have you encountered a trip to Abilene in your congregation? If so, what was the result?
- ➢ Who uses debate strategies in your congregation? Why?
- ➢ Who in your congregation is skilled in using dialogue?
- ➢ What congregational issues need a dialogic approach right now? Why?
- ➢ Who is silent in your congregation? Why?

11

COMMITMENT: IT'S NOT WHAT YOU THINK

Congregational members place a very high value on being committed. This value is appropriate since congregations, as voluntary associations (see Chapter 2), especially depend on the commitment of members if anything is to get done. Without the commitment of members there are no ministries, finances become difficult, and worship services struggle. It's common, especially in congregations experiencing decline to hear laments such as: "Young people just aren't as committed as they should be," or "If only people were more committed." Commitment becomes the obvious solution for whatever difficulty the congregation experiences. If we could somehow fix commitment, the congregation would return to its former growing state. Pastors are encouraged to preach strongly on commitment so that people will renew their vows to the congregation and the group will prosper again.

Some of this concern about commitment is appropriate. Christine Pohl notes how the current difficulty in keeping commitments generally in our culture bubbles over into our congregations.[42] Most leaders are very familiar with those who say they'll come, they'll lead, or they'll contribute but fail to show up. Ministries suffer, as do the relatively few people who seem to always shoulder the work in a congregation. Thus, what we experience in many congregations is the over-commitment of some, the free-loading of others, and the near absence of many on the rolls, which is not healthy for anyone involved.

In our personal lives we all experience the pressure of competing commitments and the struggle of sorting them out. Some of us are better than others at this task, but everyone finds it difficult. We also know how we feel when someone doesn't keep a commitment to us. Sometimes in our own lives we echo our congregations by saying "If only people were more committed."

Yet commitment is complicated. We use the term to mean a variety of actions and beliefs. We can think we agree about what it is and what it involves but a closer look reveals that we don't. Those working for change tend to be highly committed, at least to their topic. Thus, the issues surrounding commitment have a direct effect on the health of those enacting change.

Committed to What?

We experience commitment as a type of internal force that binds us to something, someone, or a course of action.[43] The focus of our commitment is called a target. For example, a target may be a belief system, a political group, a spouse, a work group, or changing a law. Given that there are different types of targets we always need to understand to what people are actually committed. When we understand the target of commitment we may understand motivations for change and responses to change as well.

Although we agree that people should be committed to their congregations, what are their actual targets of commitment? Some people are committed to the organization itself, to the congregation as an entity. This kind of commitment is very common and is perhaps most common in some of the most tireless congregational workers. If this target of commitment is the case you may hear people state, "I'm committed to making this church grow." Or "I'm committed to getting this church back on its feet." Or, when speaking of decline and the possibility of closure, flatly state, "Not on my watch." People committed to the congregation show up to make sure things work. Many of them have shown up for years.

Similarly, people may be committed to their denomination. If that is the case you may hear, "I'm [denomination] through and through and will be one no matter what." Sometimes these people serve on denominational boards and become deeply involved in denominational politics since sustaining the denomination is the target of their commitment. While they may still attend worship locally, the bulk of their energy is directed away from their congregation.

Other people are strongly committed to having the right beliefs or maintaining doctrine or ideals. They know what they believe and what you believe and how these differ. Since the target of commitment is actually the belief system, these people will leave when the belief system is disrupted. Sometimes this disruption can be over seemingly small differences in theology. Or, they may have accommodated a mismatch with their beliefs for some time and the new proposed change is just the last straw. Some research shows that those most committed to ideals and beliefs are also more likely to switch congregations.[44]

A related target is being committed to a particular action. In congregations some people are committed to achieving a goal, such as enacting social justice, participating in immigration issues, or engaging in prolife activities. All of their energy revolves around the social changes they are trying to enact

On the other hand, people may be committed to particular members or to the small group they belong to within the congregation. Rather than being committed to the organization as a whole, they are relationally driven. They really could care less about what the denomination or congregation does regarding structure, doctrine, or direction as long as they are able to maintain their relationships. If these relationships are disrupted these people will act to maintain those relationships. Sometimes choirs or other music programs serve as this type of relational commitment. This trait is revealed when changes are proposed to the music program and a firestorm erupts. Or, perhaps a small group ministry is disrupted and again major turmoil occurs. In these cases, it's not the structure or the music, it's the relationships that are truly valued.

Sometimes people are committed to an individual. If that individual is the pastor or the youth director, these people will be highly committed as long as the pastor or youth director remains and leave or become less active when he or she resigns. This result is most common in youth groups. Youth become highly committed to a youth director and fall away in his or her absence. Thus, youth groups often cycle up and down as youth directors arrive and leave, with each new youth director needing to rebuild the group.

A special case of being committed to an individual is when someone is committed primarily to God. In that case, people will move to deepen their relationship with God but may not be particularly attached to the congregation. They may belong to groups outside of the congregation that they believe support their spiritual life. Or, they may push on the congregation as a whole to provide more opportunities for spiritual growth.

Thus, the wise response to, "People need to be more committed" is to ask, "Committed to what?" It's an important question because each target will foster different responses. Although people can be committed to several targets at once, they will honor the primary target under stress. Typically, it's those committed organizationally to the congregation who bemoan the lack of commitment the loudest and with good reason. They carry most of the day-to-day work. Yet it's important to understand that even in a smaller, more cohesive group like a congregation commitment targets vary widely. Understanding to what people are committed helps everyone navigate change. Along with these different targets are different types or levels of commitment.

How Committed Are You?

Just as there are different targets of commitment, there are also different types or mindsets of commitment.[45] Affective commitment generates a strong emotional attachment and identification with the target. It's the strongest of all types of commitment. In affective commitment one deeply resonates with the mission or values or ideals of the target. For example, people may have joined a congregation because they strongly agree with what the congregation embodies. They will work tirelessly to help the congregation achieve the mission they identify with.

Normative commitment is similar to a sense of loyalty or obligation. It's somewhat weaker than affective commitment. Within a congregation, many people operate out of a sense of loyalty or obligation. They may not resonate with a mission or ministry but they think it should happen so they participate. Further, some theologies actively support obligation or duty as the foundation for a Christian life. Thus, for some, normative commitment is what the Christian life is about.

It's fairly common to find affective and normative commitment existing together, especially within congregations. Many of us resonate with some aspect of the congregation but also function out of obligation or loyalty to ensure activities or ministries happen.

Continuance commitment is the third type and the weakest of all. People who are committed this way are constantly assessing the risks and benefits of remaining. They are always looking for a better situation. If the situation becomes difficult they will leave since there was little holding them there.

The Dark Side of Commitment

Commitment is vital for sustaining congregations, relationships, and the world. Yet commitment is not always a positive attribute. The many faces of commitment have a large impact on the health of those enacting change.

The type or mindset of commitment can help or hurt those working for change, depending on the situation. In positive situations, being affectively and/or normatively committed to whatever your target is leads to greater well-being. Strongly resonating with groups, goals, and actions supports positive change, belonging, and good relationships. These types of commitment also enable one to persist in less than ideal circumstances. Since all groups eventually encounter difficulties, being able to weather them is important. Working for change is hard work and commitment enables people to persist.[46]

However, those working for change, focused on their goals, can persist too long. They work hard to address the situation, keep their obligations, and refuse to quit. Persisting, no matter what, becomes a badge of courage. Yet in long-term difficult situations those who are affectively and/or normatively committed are more prone to burnout. Ironically, it's the people engaged in continuance commitment who do best in difficult situations since they will leave before they burnout because they are constantly assessing risk and benefit.[47] It appears that those most committed may be able to see only potential benefits and are unable to assess personal, spiritual, or organizational risk. They ignore the warning signs that all is not well and the costs are too high. The risks of burnout are serious with people encountering personal and marital difficulties, choosing to leave church, and sometimes leaving the faith altogether. And, burnout can take a long time to recover from and some never really do. Thus, it's vital that in difficult situations change agents constantly assess how healthy they are and give themselves permission to pull back if they believe burnout is likely.

Another difficulty is that people can be committed to sunk costs regarding their issue. They've already used much time and energy being committed. They believe if they were to leave their commitment, they would lose that investment. In truth, they lost their time and energy at the time they spent it, not at the time they chose to release their commitment. Yet this wrong belief can cause people to persevere long after it's healthy for them.

Congregational decline also poses a special risk for the committed. Many of the most stalwart workers in a congregation are strongly organizationally committed. Leaders and members count on them anytime something needs to be done. They have often worked tirelessly over decades so that the congregation or ministry can prosper. Obviously, they are affectively and/or normatively committed since they have been able to cheerfully persist for so long and through so many challenges. However, when a congregation moves into decline, these are the people who suffer the deepest. They are watching decades of sacrifice unravel before their eyes. They don't understand that working harder will not address decline, nor will doing what they've always done, but somehow better. They have a deep commitment but lack the skills needed for a different reality. Their responses, based in the past, are wrong.

One of the difficulties is that these members locate the problem in others' lack. They maintain the root of a problem is that others should be more faithful, rather than considering that others may understand commitment differently, not value the same activities in the same way, or be experiencing life challenges. They fail to understand that congregational life and members' needs have changed. Rather than opening a dialogue on commitment and what it means to all members, they resort to blaming those who don't measure up. As you listen to these people, others' lack of commitment is a constant theme. They are frustrated and feel somehow betrayed. They believe that if others were committed there would be no problem. Thus, commitment becomes the technical fix to a large adaptive challenge (see Chapter 6). As a result, it's not uncommon to find those who have been the most stalwart to also be the most opposed to working through the adaptive challenges inherent in decline. The commitment that has sustained them as well as the congregation now becomes everyone's worst enemy.

Working Wisely with Commitment

If those working for change are to persist in healthy ways they need to clearly understand their own commitments. What are the actual targets? How strong are those commitments? The following table allows you to begin to explore your actual commitments related to your congregation. You may need to expand or adjust it to fit your own situation.

	Congregation	Ideals	Actions (define)	Relationships
Affective commitment				
Normative commitment				
Mixed normative and affective				
Continuance commitment				

Figure 11.1: Mapping commitments

When you have honestly charted your various commitments in your congregation, it is also helpful to map your commitments at work and with your family. Given all your commitments, how are you managing to balance them? Are your commitments leading toward a healthy life? Are you overloaded in one area? Overloaded in all? Where is there risk of burnout?

I can't overemphasize the risk of burnout. The stakes are high. Most of us believe we are stronger and can shoulder more than we are actually able to over time. While we live in a society that devalues long-term commitment we also live in a society that overvalues busyness and productivity. Thus, we tend to overload ourselves, often without thinking. We can become so (seemingly) adept at keeping all the balls in the air that we fail to recognize how we and our most important relationships are beginning to fail. Sometimes it's important to step away for a time to reflect about one's commitments.

The take away

➤ Commitment is multi-faceted. Thus, we need to understand to what we are committed and how strongly.
➤ Commitment has a dark side, which can lead to burnout in those most committed.

Taking it further

➤ To what do your congregational leaders want you to be committed? Why?

➤ How do they support these commitments?

➤ How is the term "commitment" used as a metaphor for another congregational issue?

➤ If you honestly map your commitments, how healthy are you?

SECTION THREE

BEING SMART ABOUT CARING FOR YOURSELF

Being a change agent in a congregation can be tough. It takes persistence, creativity, wisdom, and strength of character. It's easy to lose your way in the midst of enacting change since the pressures can be very great. Burnout is always a strong possibility. Those who become burned-out often leave their congregation and sometimes their faith as well so self-understanding and self-care are vital. This section explores different aspects of self-care for those enacting congregational change.

> ➤ Chapter 12 provides perspectives for staying healthy as a change agent.
> ➤ Chapter 13 offers strategies for women change agents.

12

STRADDLING TWO WORLDS

Do you know a person that in some important ways doesn't really fit in their congregation? Perhaps they've had different life experiences than most. Or, they may hold differing beliefs about significant topics in their denomination. Perhaps they experience their walk of faith differently than others. Or, their passion for their specific call to serve God isn't reflected in the rest of the congregation. Yet there are also many values and beliefs of their congregation or denomination with which they do resonate. They can't imagine not being Catholic or Presbyterian or Baptist.

Actually, they inhabit two worlds simultaneously and have two identities they work to honor. Both identities are important; they would not be healthy without them since these identities are authentically who they are. Indeed, for them to live as a person of integrity, they must honor these conflicting beliefs. For many working for change, this experience of not really fitting in, of straddling two worlds, and of attempting to live with integrity as they manage conflicting values, is a reality they live with every day.

People who continue to remain in a group when their values conflict with it in some significant way are called tempered radicals.[48] Common examples of tempered radicals in the workplace include women within traditionally male professions or minorities within traditionally White institutions. In these examples, tempered radicals work to honor their gender and/or ethnic values simultaneously with their organizational or professional values. Tempered radicals often appear as loyal company employees on the outside, yet are different internally, based on their conflicting values. These conflicting values form the foundation for conflicting identities since our value commitments help construct our identity. It is the struggle to enact these conflicting identities that is at the heart of tempered radicals' experience. Tempered radicals are not chameleons, exhibiting one identity here and another there. Nor do they lack integrity or authenticity. Indeed, their integrity and authenticity are revealed as they work to honor both identities simultaneously.

Understanding Tempered Radicals

Tempered radicals exist in business, medicine, education, and also in denominations and congregations. As with tempered radicals in other areas, those in congregations are very aware that fitting in with congregational or denominational values and beliefs contradicts who they are. They struggle with managing the officially sanctioned identity of "good Catholic," "good Christian" or "good member" that conflicts with their own values on how to live out their faith. Tempered radicals' issues vary with person and situation. Some may focus on actually "walking the talk" in social justice issues or working to live with integrity. Others may long for expanded participation and roles for women and/or laity. Still others may long for truly authentic practices of faith rather than the sometimes shallow busyness of congregational life. Yet tempered radicals are not defined so much by their issues as by what makes them tick.[49]

Tempered radicals tend to be primarily committed to a deep connection with God, rather than being committed to a congregation or a denomination. With this foundation, tempered radicals view their faith relationally. While they know the doctrines and policies of their denomination, often as well as the pastor, their faith does not rest in doctrine or official statements. Instead, it rests on a living relationship with God and they often speak of God in the same way they would speak of a close friend. For them, God matters far more than anything else. Loving and obeying God fuels how they live their lives. Yet with this orientation toward their faith, congregational life and denominational emphases can often feel shallow or misplaced. Congregational busyness and business become a source of frustration as people refuse to "walk the talk" or engage in practices leading toward a deeper expression of what it means to be Christian.

Tempered radicals also tend to be deeply oriented toward ministry arising out of calling and gifting rather than requirements of position, education, and gender. They truly understand that the fields are ready to harvest and the workers are few.[50] They are ready to work in their chosen arena and strongly object to "*you* can't because . . . ," especially when vital ministry will be left undone. They see the discrepancy between a call to serve God with their gifts and practices that exclude or discourage their participation because of what they are *not* rather than who they *are*. Indeed, my own research shows that tempered radicals keenly feel these barriers. They view them as inauthentic, unjust, and wasting God's resources in a world always in need of grace.

Tempered radicals are also people of vision. Since they straddle the worlds of "now and not yet" they see what could be in the midst of what is. These visions are not top-down, easily aligning with denominational or congregational direction, but arise from the heart of the person. Instead, their vision is aligned with creating a space for their calling, whether it's social justice, integrity, authentic transformation, gender equality, or other issues. Each is deeply committed to his or her vision; it is who he or she is. Often, everything radicals choose to do will center around their vision, since they believe it is how God has called them to live out their faith and minister to others. They will pursue this vision in spite of the lack of support they receive from those around them.

Tempered radicals can seem similar to dissidents, but their approach of quiet, incremental change and choosing to remain within the congregation make them different. They can also seem like the informal leaders that congregations so depend on. Yet informal leaders usually don't have a strong experience of not fitting in. Indeed, it is because they do fit in that informal leaders are so effective. Nor are tempered radicals like true radicals. They differ because they are tempered. This tempering has several facets. First, tempered radicals tend to seek moderation, rather than quick, disruptive change. They have also learned to endure, so they are tough. Yet they are also passionate and will not let things go on without comment or action.[51]

Tempered radicals tend to be quiet, working behind the scenes to create space for who they are and what they care about rather than openly dissenting. They often use incremental methods to work for change, rather than pushing for large transformative change. They have learned to work creatively and, most of all, patiently, as they honor both parts of their identity. In short, they are those who remain loyal to their congregation or denomination but also listen to a decidedly different voice. They live in the tension of what is now and what could be. It is living in this tension that makes their lives so challenging.

Challenges of Tempered Radicals

Living in tension, enduring what is the current reality while seeing what could, and often should, be in a congregation is emotionally wearing. Struggling to honor one's call from God in a group that ignores it or opposes it is wearying. Desiring support for ministry while not receiving it is discouraging. Thus, tempered radicals have an uphill battle. Indeed, few people actively choose to be a tempered radical, but instead find this life thrust upon them as they try to authentically honor who they are within a congregation that often doesn't. Most healthy people work to resolve strong emotional tension like this by leaving a group or devaluing a group. But this strategy doesn't work for tempered radicals since they have chosen to remain with their congregation. They have chosen to be committed and in many ways they are the most committed of all since they endure such discomfort by remaining.

This long-standing and strong emotional tension makes tempered radicals prone to burnout over time. Their experience of not really fitting in is particularly difficult in a congregation since most congregations like to portray themselves as friendly, peaceful, and supportive places to be. Since the congregation is often a source of deep frustration, tempered radicals get a double dose. They can't access the support others so easily do. They can't fit in and then they are told they should feel like they fit in and should be happy about it!

As you might expect, tempered radicals can feel a lot of (often) internalized anger as well as guilt about who they are. They may also feel like failures since it's difficult to honor both identities and conflicting values well all the time. And, as you might expect, tempered radicals can feel pretty lonely and isolated. Like the rest of us, they want to be in a place where they truly feel at home. For tempered radicals, those places are difficult to find. Realistically, they most likely won't find them within their congregation. Further, like other types of dissidents in congregations, they reap the common consequences of seeing things differently. Tempered radicals, even though they are quiet and moderate, can be devalued, ignored, or openly shunned (see Chapter 8).

Yet in spite of these significant challenges many tempered radicals are quite successful as persistent agents of change in their congregations. Their persistence is anchored in several practices that sustain them over time.

Sustaining Tempered Radicals

My own research explored how tempered radicals persist in congregations. How do they continue to live positive, faith-filled lives? As I interviewed successful tempered radicals I learned that they engage in several sustaining practices.

A first step toward being a successful tempered radical is to actually own that it's true. Recognizing that one is experiencing this reality does much to relieve the sense of failure, frustration, and guilt that tempered radicals so often face. It also can refine their commitment to their congregation. They have actually chosen to remain in a situation where they don't fit. They do have other options, even though they may not recognize them. Knowing that it has been a conscious choice on their part to remain and that other options may be available allows them to consider why and how they remain committed where they are (see Chapter 11).

Second, successful tempered radicals surround themselves with supportive relationships. They realize that the congregation or a single group will not be able to support them fully. Thus, they seek out groups that sustain their different identities. For example, someone may be worshipping regularly in one congregation but actively serving in a social justice area with a different group or congregation. Or, perhaps someone regularly attends two widely differing worship services, such as a contemplative or alternative service at one congregation and a more traditional service at another.

Alternately, tempered radicals can surround themselves with like-minded people. For example, they develop friendships that support different parts of their identity. These friendships allow them to be who they are some of the time and to explore different ideas. However, none of this happens automatically so tempered radicals need to actively create this relational support. It offsets the isolation and loneliness that tempered radicals feel as well as supporting them as they work for change.

Many tempered radicals have vibrant role models, living and dead, that they find sustaining. Some draw on denominational heroes since many of them were open dissidents or tempered radicals themselves. Many founders of Protestant churches exhibit this trait. Becoming familiar with their life-stories and meditating on their struggles can be deeply encouraging. Others draw solace from the lives of saints, who again were often dissidents or tempered radicals. Still others meditate on the lives of heroes in the Bible. Some tempered radicals have been fortunate to have had living mentors that they can draw upon as well.

Successful tempered radicals have also learned how to pick their battles wisely. They have a strong sense of vision and can recognize what activities support that vision and which do not. Since they are part of the congregation, they learn to recognize when they are pushing too hard or are generating a backlash. They most often focus on small, incremental change. On the one hand, this strategy works well since it gives the congregation time to adapt. However, it can be difficult for the tempered radical since they can see where the group needs to go while the pace of change can seem glacially slow.

Obviously, since tempered radicals tend to experience God relationally, taking the time and energy to attend to that relationship is vital. It's easy in the pressures of life to ignore spending time with God. However, God, most of all, understands the lives tempered radicals lead and wise tempered radicals develop this relationship. For many tempered radicals, entering into spiritual direction or developing trusted friends they can openly share their spiritual lives with supports developing a stronger relationship with God.

How Congregations Can Welcome Tempered Radicals

In congregations experiencing change or decline, tempered radicals should be a treasured resource. They see the world differently and have different ideas. They can offer a prophetic witness to the complacency and inwardness of congregational life. They can challenge members to deepen and expand their walks of faith. They provide bridges to other groups who wish to belong, but can't or won't until something changes. Tempered radicals can make difficult congregational or denominational changes easier since they may embody the direction the group needs to move. They can be a gift to a congregation, supporting change and authentic Christianity. However, all too often tempered radicals lead lives of quiet desperation and their gifts fall by the wayside. Thus, creating a supportive environment is important if the congregation wants to reap the benefits.

First, implementing any or all of the suggestions in Chapter 8 regarding dissent improves the situation for tempered radicals. Second, since tempered radicals are often fruitful members of the congregation, it's appropriate that they should be entitled to some level of pastoral support. That support could include providing spiritual direction or directing them to supportive relationships. Pastors should be aware of the potential for burnout and encourage tempered radicals to step away from ministry as needed. Support could also include understanding that tempered radicals are not necessarily being disloyal to the congregation when they pursue relationships or opportunities outside of it. Indeed, encouraging tempered radicals to broaden their relational base ensures they can remain within the congregation long-term.

Finally, since tempered radicals feel the barriers preventing their ministry so keenly, wise leaders will consider which of these barriers are actually necessary. Many of these barriers are invisible except to those who experience them regularly. Perhaps some ways of relating to God are devalued or women or laity aren't allowed to minister even though denominational policies don't openly forbid it. Or, congregational members whisper about someone's ministry outside of the congregation. Wise leaders will work with their tempered radicals so they can involve them in their chosen arena. They can try to remove those invisible barriers. They can develop work-around strategies so tempered radicals can serve and be honored for their service. Finally, as much as possible they can advocate for them within the congregation and denomination.

The take away

➤ Tempered radicals are change agents whose values are in conflict in some significant way with those of their congregation. They straddle two worlds.
➤ They can work effectively for change, especially if they engage in sustaining practices.
➤ Congregations can reap the benefits of tempered radicals' ministry as they work to create a supportive environment.

Taking it further

➤ Do you identify yourself as a tempered radical? If so, why? If not, who would you identify as one in your congregation?
➤ What issues do you think are important to the tempered radicals in your congregation?
➤ If you are a tempered radical, what challenges do you specifically face? What sustaining practices have you found to be effective?

> ➤ How could you be more supportive of the tempered radicals in your congregation? What specific steps could your congregation take?

13

WISDOM FOR WOMEN

The earlier chapters of this book have addressed all manner of people working for change: dissidents, tempered radicals, Catholics, Protestants, those who are progressive, and those who are conservative in theology. However, what I haven't done is addressed gender issues. Yet women face special challenges when enacting change. This chapter will explore some of those challenges as well as some possible avenues for managing them.

Women form the majority in nearly all congregations. Women may be more drawn to the relational life embodied in congregations. They can feel more responsible for the spiritual nurture of their children and so become involved. They also live longer so it's common to have more elderly women in a congregation than elderly men.

Without the endless hours women volunteer, congregational life would come to a standstill. And, while the level of women's volunteerism has declined as more women have entered the workforce, women still make congregational life happen in countless ways, large and small. Many men entering into congregational leadership understand that they must become adept at working with (and often, for) women. Indeed, one of the old jokes about what qualifies a man to be a pastor is that he must like to listen to women talk!

Yet what occurs in many congregations is that while women do the majority of the work and make up over half of the congregation they often have little official voice. In conservative Protestant congregations women are not allowed in leadership positions, based on both tradition and interpretations of some New Testament texts. In Catholic parishes, lay men can have more clout than lay women or even women religious (nuns), with all laity residing under the authority of a strong male hierarchy. Even within more progressive congregations, women's voices may be devalued based on congregational culture. Until the last 50 or 60 years, women were not allowed to learn, teach, or write on theological matters in many denominations. Thus, issues that directly concerned women were often invisible simply because male leaders were largely unaware of women's experience and their perspectives. While women now have more theological voice in many denominations and women's experience and perspectives are more welcome, congregational culture and power structures can still prefer men and men's ways of seeing the world. And, as I noted at the beginning of the book, culture is difficult to change.

Thus, when women enact change they have a double dilemma. Change is unpopular coming from anyone and women's voices are less heard and less valued. To further complicate matters, many issues that interest change agents are seen as women's issues: gender equity, care for the poor (who are often single women with children or elderly women), care for children, and increasing the emotional content of worship. Let's look a little more at some specific challenges.

Challenges for Women

When women work for change they are more likely to be called marginal members than men working for change. When change is threatening, one strategy of disarming change agents is to argue that they attend infrequently or aren't really important in other ways to the congregation. In short, why would we listen to someone who hardly ever comes? However, many women change agents attend worship regularly, serve on committees, and contribute in other significant ways.[52] Women working for change are also more likely to have their efforts labeled as obstruction (relational conflict, see Chapter 7), faithless, and as fueling special interest politics. In contrast, men advocating for the same changes may be labeled as leaders, Spirit-led, or as following God.[53]

A related challenge is that assertive women can be viewed negatively. Enacting change means that you have to be assertive, even if quietly assertive, in some fashion. Yet when women are considered for available leadership positions, they can be seen as too assertive or too soft, with nothing in the middle. Strong women are denigrated and culturally acceptable female behavior is seen as not appropriate for leadership. This situation is called the double bind in the workplace.

In denominations that do support women in leadership, women still often work within a framework of male leadership practices. In the US, leadership is defined by male attributes.[54] If you are a good leader, pastoral or lay, you will embody male behaviors, such as assertiveness, rationality, individuality, and power posturing and dismiss behaviors that seem more feminine, such as collaboration, intuitive approaches, and relationship-building. Thus, particularly within conservative Protestant congregations, women must learn to function within this male framework to be effective, although much of congregational life benefits from a more "feminine" approach.

Further, various generations understand what it means to be a "good Christian woman" differently.[55] Elderly women often view the congregation as an extension of their own household and engage in housekeeping for God. They tend to be spiritually passive, gladly receiving what is offered by leaders. They value altar guilds, cooking, sewing, and cleaning. These practices are spiritually significant to these women and they are frustrated that younger women don't engage in them.

Mid-life women, who have come through the changes in women's roles in society, often want leadership and gender equity within the congregation. Even when that desire may not be achievable, they wish to be openly honored for what they contribute. They are also more assertive in what they long for spiritually, asking for different types of worship services and retreats.

Younger women are less invested in traditional ways of being a Christian woman. With careers and family they are interested in creating a spirituality that supports their whole life. They will still contribute to the congregation, but they want it to be in meaningful, rather than traditional, ways.

With these broad generational attributes in mind, it's easy to see that not all women will see change the same way. Nor will typical women's issues play out the same for all women in the congregation. Indeed, the handoff of congregational women's work between generations is often a very rocky one with frustration for all involved.

A woman tempered radical I interviewed spoke eloquently on the difficulties of handing off women's responsibilities within her congregation. Although she and her associates were in their 40s they were just now being allowed to take on most of the responsibilities. There was a fair amount of frustration on both sides during this process. The older and younger women did not understand each others' values and experiences easily and there were often hurt feelings all around.

To explore this potential for conflict a little further, younger women, with children and careers, may not value weekly or monthly meetings to discuss small points. Yet these meetings are very significant for older women who often have a long history of meeting this way. Nor do younger women want to meet during the day since they are working or have to arrange childcare. Older women value the relational support these planning meetings provide and don't want to meet at night. Older women remember why decisions were made, often decades ago, and these decisions may not make sense to younger women since the world has changed. The potential frustration points are many as women hand off women's work and sometimes women are not kind to one another in the process.

Enacting change requires a lot of emotional energy. Especially if one is a tempered radical, emotional energy can be at a premium since not fitting in is emotionally wearing. Yet women often engage in emotionally draining work outside of their congregations. They are more apt to be in caring professions and many still perform most childcare. It's easy for women to emotionally spend more than their emotional resources support, which leads to burnout.

A woman's choices on pursuing gender issues can also make it more difficult for her to find supportive relationships as she works for change. For example, feminist women may view Catholicism or conservative Protestantism as abusive to women. Women who remain in these congregations can be seen by feminists outside as not honoring their own gender. A feminist Catholic or conservative Protestant may be shunned inside the congregation and within secular feminist groups as well. For women tempered radicals, gender provides another challenge in their already stressful situations.

Finally, for women change agents in congregations, navigating gender is always on the plate, which is not usually the case for men. If women wish to be active with other change initiatives they must decide whether and how to add gender issues to the mix. Since the dominant congregational culture is often male, males working for change rarely feel any pressure to address gender. Their choices are simpler and it is easier to pick battles and moderate the emotional energy it takes to work for change. If women decline to pursue gender issues in favor of other change as a way to manage emotional energy, other women may take offense since gender equity is such an important topic.

Help along the Way

In my research I interviewed women tempered radicals. I am a lay tempered radical as well. Based on my interviews and my own experience, I would like to offer some ways to manage the challenges specific to women.

First, since gender is such a large issue for women, it is well worth the time to thoroughly understand the role it plays in one's own role as a change agent. Women can't escape gender in their work for change and clearly understanding one's stance regarding women's roles and why one holds it will lessen some of frustration. For example, if you are not pursuing gender equity in your congregation it helps to develop a specific script explaining why that is not the case since it will be questioned by possible supporters.

Second, I cannot overemphasize the importance of finding supportive relationships. Realistically, the congregation may not be able to provide the types of sustaining relationships a woman will need, especially if she struggles to fit in as a tempered radical. Ironically, in a place where one should feel most at home women, in particular, can instead feel strongly alienated.[56] If one is a tempered radical one should cultivate relationships that explicitly support the different identities and look broadly for them.

There are several options for finding supportive relationships while remaining in a congregation. In a larger congregation there may be others interested in the same issues. Choosing to align along the issue rather than along gender may give women male allies. Male allies can prove important within conservative Protestant and Catholic congregations and women do well to remember that many men would also welcome gender equity. Meeting with kindred spirits regularly outside the congregation to honestly discuss challenges can help. Alternately, many denominations have dissident groups on certain issues that one can join. However, dissident groups should be treated with caution. Dissident groups can end up becoming one's true congregation. While this reality feels good, it means that there are less resources for change in the original congregation, since one's heart and energy are invested elsewhere.

Third, it's also important to choose the battles and strategies wisely. Emotional energy is at a premium and the strain of dealing constantly with gender issues and/or male ways of doing business lessens it further. One strategy is to specifically limit the number of issues, or the manifestation of those issues, upon which to focus. This strategy is why some women don't add addressing gender issues to their slate. For example, they may be keenly interested in ministering to the poor and advocating explicitly for gender equity in the congregation would overwhelm their resources. Another strategy is to work for a series of small, incremental wins. The energy needed is low but consistent and the impacts of failure are lessened so it becomes easier to recover. Small wins also generate less resistance in the larger group and can build on each other. However, the pace of change with a small wins strategy is slow, which can prove frustrating.

Women, in particular, can benefit from learning to enact dissent effectively. They should be especially vigilant about keeping their dissent as task conflict. Women's dissent is routinely assessed negatively and the double bind is always functioning. Entering into relational conflict will only fuel these negative assessments. Women need to become skilled at moving relational conflict back into task conflict or walking away when unable to do so (see Chapter 6).

The take away

➢ Women change agents have much to offer their congregations but they meet many challenges specific to women.
➢ These many challenges can be lessened by understanding and practicing dissent wisely and finding support along the way.

Taking it further

➢ How are women change agents viewed in your congregation? Why?
➢ If you are a woman change agent, how do you manage gender as you advocate for change? What's been helpful? If you are a male change agent, what role does gender play for you?
➢ If you have decided to lay aside gender issues in favor of other important issues, how do you explain that decision to others? If you have decided to keep gender on your plate, why?
➢ How carefully do you manage your emotional resources?

14

Some Final Thoughts on Being Smart

In this book I've offered numerous perspectives on congregations and change as well as practical ways to implement change. I would like to offer some final guidance about how to be smart about change in any situation.

Building a Bridge

The first section of this book focused on different ways to understand your congregation. As I noted at the beginning, each of these ways are interrelated, but together they create a coherent picture of the congregation. The reason for this emphasis on knowing your congregation is that enacting change involves building a bridge for people to walk on into the future. One side of this bridge is anchored in the future you are trying to reach. The other side of the bridge is anchored in the past. In the present, people are walking on the bridge as you build it. Wisely enacting change means that you are able to anchor your change in the past and to do that you need to know what the past is. The proposed change has to make sense in the present if people are to move into the future. If it doesn't make sense people can't move forward.

Many change initiatives fail at this point. Leaders and visionaries can be gifted at seeing the future, but fail to appreciate the effects of congregational culture, narrative, and spirituality while trying to get to that future. I urge you to know your congregation well *before* embarking on a major change initiative. Work to anchor the change in the past and have it make sense in the present. If you are unable to do so, you should probably rethink your change initiative.

Appreciating Difference

First, I should note that the term *difference* is sometimes used as a code word. Accommodating difference is often a path toward changing denominational stances on human sexuality. I am not using the term in that way. Instead, I am maintaining that people differ in many significant ways, even within a congregation. Learning to appreciate those differences and welcome differing perspectives makes enacting change easier.

As I've talked with laity and leaders of congregations in decline, I've been struck by how many of them are unable to work with even small differences in practices, beliefs, and styles. And, congregations in decline are not the only ones unable to manage these types of difference, it's just most pronounced in them. Congregations can quickly become set in their ways. They easily develop strong unspoken rules about practices and beliefs that often have little to do with historical Christian or denominational theology and practice. These congregations welcome the few "people like us" and exclude the many "not like us." The problem is that those "not like us" include faithful Christians who may be from different socioeconomic, political, ethnic, or educational backgrounds. Or, perhaps they have had different religious experiences or they may have a sense of call toward a ministry that is not valued by the congregation. Whatever the difference, congregations rigidly maintain their boundaries of "like us" and can be quite inhospitable toward the "not like us." All too often, congregations choose to try to fit everyone in the same mold, arguing Christianity is a narrow set of rigidly enforced practices and beliefs.

Change initiatives often arise from those on margins and from the "not like us" people. When these change initiatives arise, congregations can chose to discern whether God is leading them in a new direction. Or, they can slam the door on change since the initiative arises from difference. Congregations with a practice of appreciating difference can be more open to considering change. They experience less threat from new ideas or different perspectives.

Appreciating difference is not easy. Congregations need to be constantly encouraged to practice a holy hospitality toward other believers, especially those who are different in some way. This holy hospitality toward others also enlarges ministry and welcomes unbelievers. I urge you to observe how your congregation appreciates difference. If it has become rigid, the first step toward change maybe to explore how the "like us" people actually differ from one another.

Practicing Change

Many of us have heard the phrase "we don't want change for change's sake." Certainly, being in a constantly changing environment, especially when those changes are deep and/or stressful is difficult for anyone. However, being in an environment that doesn't change isn't good either, since we gradually (or not so gradually) become rigid and unable to change at all. Thus, we do want "change for change's sake" so that when we need to change we are able to. We want to always be in an environment where some level of change is occurring.

Some people see their congregation as a change-free zone. Scripture says God doesn't change and some forms of liturgy have remained essentially the same for centuries or even millennia. The Bible remains the same. Some liturgies state a variation of, "As it was in the beginning, is now and will be forever. Amen." It can be easy for people to slip into believing that while change runs rampant in the culture it can't cross the threshold of the church. And, some people are self-appointed guards, ensuring that change doesn't arise in their congregation or ministry.

While having a change-free zone can feel comfortable and safe, it's not healthy, since it leads to rigidity. A change-free zone is actually an illusion. Change is always occurring in a congregation. People come and go. Pastors come and go. People change and as they change the congregation changes with them. The congregational lifecycle continues to run. Thus, the question becomes how to work wisely with change.

The key idea in working with change is to understand that change is like exercise. If you don't use it, you lose it. In other words, a continuous level of small change enables people to more easily accommodate larger changes. Those larger changes are unavoidable. Unfortunately, the largest and most difficult changes of all, those associated with deep decline, often come to the most rigid congregations. Indeed, their rigidity is one factor fueling their decline. Thus, I would urge you to welcome change for change's sake. Not deep, continuous, radical change, but a consistent, moderate level of change. It will enable the congregation to face those coming larger changes wisely. Flexibility takes practice.

A Final Thought

Some have claimed that we are experiencing a time of the felt absence of God in our culture. Others maintain that we are going through a major social transition that only happens every few centuries. I tend to agree with both of these assertions. Whether you agree or not, it seems that our culture and our congregations are having a very tough time. I expect these challenging times to last into the foreseeable future.

Yet no matter how challenging the times are, God is present. At times it can be hard to see what God is doing and how God is building the Church, especially when many congregations are in decline or struggling in other ways. It's good to remember that before the new can spring forth, the old must die. God is active in the living, the dying, and the rebuilding of the Church. God is always faithful.

ACKNOWLEDGMENTS

In many ways I've been writing this book for much of my life, which makes it hard to even begin to recognize those who helped in creating it. Every congregation I've attended has contributed in ways large and small. Many authors have contributed to my worldview as have countless conversations. So please recognize that the following is a very incomplete list. That said, I would like to specifically honor those named below.

Dr. Sandra Wilson, Dr. Jeannette Abi-Nader, and Dr. Mary Garvin (deceased) for their passion for congregational change and their enthusiasm for writing for laity rather than only for academics.

Ann Kramp for helping me recognize my passion and Diana Stoffregen for her wise guidance over many years.

Pastors Larry Cudmore, Dudley Nolting, Paul Bodin, Erik Samuelson, Ed Pace, and Mike Von Behren for great discussion, support, listening, and prayer.

Dr. Merry Jo Demarais and Dr. Charlotte Lamp for forming a supportive writing group. Their encouragement and support was vital.

The following have provided much needed knowledge, wisdom, and support: Dr. Evan and Cheri Howard, Dr. Joy Milos, Dr. Linda Schearing, Dr. James Dallen, Dr. David Whitfield, Dr. Shann Ferch, Dr. James Beebe, Lynn Affeldt, Gail Gutterud, Jim Keizer, Nancy Larson-Powers, Marsha Olsen, Beth Nolting, and Carla Roland.

I would like to thank my family: Dr. Anna Zemke, Nathan and Alaina Zemke, Rev. David and Stasia Zemke, Jonathan and Katy Zemke, and Bethany and Robert Downs. In particular, Jonathan provided insights that formed the basis for my research. David read the original draft of this book and offered many astute comments and realistic feedback.

Finally, I would like to thank my husband, Dr. Steven Zemke. He has read every word and offered valuable feedback. He has also provided deep encouragement during writing as well as the support to do it.

NOTES

Chapter 1: The Past Creates the Present

[1] Schein, E. (1992). *Organizational Culture and Leadership*. 2nd ed. San Francisco: Jossey-Bass. p. 12.

[2] "Left behind." *The Economist*, Sept. 10. 2011 print edition. Downloaded from http://www.economist.com/node/21528614 on 2/14/2012.

Chapter 2: The Distinctiveness of Congregational Life

[3] Harris, M. (1998). A special case of voluntary association? Towards a theory of congregational organization. *British Journal of Sociology 49*(4), 602-618.

[4] Cameron, K. and Quinn, R. (2006). *Diagnosing and Changing Organizational Culture*. San Francisco: Jossey-Bass.

[5] Dimaggio, P. (1998). The relevance of organizational theory to the study of religion. In Demerath, N., Hall, P., Schmitt, T., and Williams, R. (eds.), *Sacred Companies*. New York: Oxford University Press, p. 8.

Chapter 3: Practicing our Faith Together

[6] Schwarz, C. and Schalk, C., (1998). *Natural Church Development*. St. Charles, IL: ChurchSmart Resources.

[7] Howard, E. (2008). *The Brazos Introduction to Christian Spirituality*. Grand Rapids, MI: Brazos Press.

[8] See Foster, R. (1978). *Celebration of Discipline*. New York: Harper and Row; Thompson, (M). (1995) *Soul Feast: An Invitation to the Christian Spiritual Life*. Louisville, KY: Westminster John Knox Press.

[9] Howard, E., pp. 28-30.

[10] Ware, C. (1995). *Discover Your Spiritual Type: A Guide to Individual and Congregational Growth*. Herndon, VA: The Alban Institute.

[11] Driskill, J. (1999). *Protestant Spiritual Exercises: Theology, History, and Practice*. Harrisburg, PA: Morehouse Publishing.

Chapter 4: What Stories Tell Us

[12] Hopewell, J. (1987). *Congregation: Stories and Structures*. Philadelphia, PA: Fortress Press.

[13] Driskill, J. (1999). *Protestant Spiritual Exercises: Theology, History, and Practice*. Harrisburg, PA: Morehouse Publishing

[14] Hopewell, p. 69.

[15] Hopewell, p. 40-41.

Chapter 5: Beginnings, Endings, and the Space Between

[16] http://money.cnn.com/magazines/fortune/fortune 500_archive/full/1955/index.html. Accessed 4/3/2012

[17] Collins, Jim (2001). *Good to Great: Why Some Companies Make the Leap and Others Don't*. New York: HarperCollins.

Chapter 6: Change as an Adaptive Challenge

[18] Gray, S. and Dumond, F. (2009). *Legacy Churches*. St. Charles, IL: ChurchSmart Resources.

[19] See Heifetz, R. (1994). *Leadership without Easy Answers*. Cambridge, MA: Belknap Press; Heifetz, R., Grashow, A., and Linsky, M. (2009). *The Practice of Adaptive Leadership*. Boston, MA: Harvard Business Press.

Chapter 7: Working with Conflict

[20] For an extended discussion of anxiety and loss in adaptive change see Heifetz, R., Grashow, A., and Linsky, M. (2009). *The Practice of Adaptive Leadership*. Boston, MA: Harvard Business Press.

[21] Steinke, P. (2006). *Congregational Leadership in Anxious Times*. Herndon, VA: The Alban Institute, pp. 107-108.

[22] Markham, D. (1999). *Spiritlinking Leadership: Working Through Resistance to Organizational Change*. New York: Paulist Press.

[23] Prentice, D., Miller, D., and Lightdale J. (2006). Asymmetries in attachments to groups and their members: Distinguishing between common-identity and common-bond groups. In J. Levine and R. Moreland (Eds.), *Small Groups* (pp. 83-95). New York: Psychology Press.

Chapter 8: Dissent is Not a Dirty Word

[24] Kassing, J. and DiCioccio, R. (2004). Testing a workplace experience explanation of displaced dissent. *Communication Reports, (17)* 2, 113-120.

[25] Nemeth, C. and Nemeth-Brown, B. (2003). Better than individuals? The potential benefits of dissent and diversity for group creativity. In P. Paulus and B. Nijstad (Eds.), *Group Creativity: Innovation through Collaboration.* (pp. 63-84). New York: Oxford.

[26] Nemeth, C. (1995). Dissent as driving cognition, attitudes and judgments. *Social Cognition, 13*(3), 273-291.

[27] Tjosvold, D. (1997). Conflict with interdependence: Its value for productivity and individuality. In C. De Creu and E. Van de Vliert (Eds.), *Using Conflict in Organizations* (pp. 23-37). Thousand Oaks, CA: Sage.

[28] Steinke, P. (2006). *Congregational Leadership in Anxious Times.* Herndon, VA: The Alban Institute, p. 108.

[29] Steinke, p. 107.

[30] These steps are derived from West, M. (2006). Dissent in teams and organizations: Lessons for team innovation and empowerment. In M. Van Lange (Ed.), *Bridging Social Psychology: Benefits of Transdisciplinary Approaches* (pp. 353-358), Mahwah, NJ: Lawrence Erlbaum.

Chapter 9: Working with Loss and Grief

[31] See, for example, MacDonald, G. *(2007).Who Stole My Church?* Dallas, TX: Thomas Nelson.

[32] See Stein, H. (2007). The inconsolable organization: Toward a theory of organization and culture change. *Psychoanalysis, Culture, and Society (12).* pp. 349-368; Stein, H. (2009) Understanding and consulting with inconsolable organizations. *Illness, Crisis, and Loss (17)*3, pp. 243-259.

[33] Stein, H. (1988). Aggression, grief-work, and organizational development: Theory and case example. *Organization Development Journal (6)* 1, pp. 22-28.

[34] Owen, H. (1986). Griefwork in organizations. *Consultation (5)*1, pp. 41-51.

131

[35] See Bridges, W. and Mitchell, S. (2008) Leading transition: A new model for change. In E. Hesselbein and A. Schrader (Eds.), *Leader to Leader 2. Jossey-Bass.* p. 246-255; Bridges, W. (1986). Managing organizational transitions. *Organizational Dynamics.* William Bridges has also written several books on managing personal and organizational transitions. See, for example, Bridges, W. (2009). *Managing Transitions,* 3rd ed. DeCapo Press.

Chapter 10: The Many Pitfalls of Decision-making

[36] Dave Arnott has explored cult-like behavior in the workplace, but the attributes extend to congregations as well. See Arnott, D. (2000). *Corporate Cults.* New York: AMACOM.

[37] Janis, I. (1982) *Groupthink: Psychological Studies of Policy Decisions and Fiascoes* (2nd ed.) Boston, MA: Houghton Mifflin.

[38] Staw, B., Sandelands, L. and Dutton, J. (1988). Threat-rigidity effects in organizational behavior: A multilevel analysis. In K. Cameron, R. Sutton and D. Whetten (Eds.), *Readings in Organizational Decline.* Cambridge, MA: Ballinger.

[39] Cameron, K., Sutton, R., and Whetten, D. (1988). Issues in organizational decline. In K. Cameron, R. Sutton and D. Whetten (Eds.), *Readings in Organizational Decline.* Cambridge, MA: Ballinger.

[40] Harvey, Jerry. (1988). *The Abilene Paradox and Other Meditations on Management.* Lexington, MA: Lexington Books.

[41] Senge, P. (1990). *The Fifth Discipline.* New York: Doubleday. p. 240.

Chapter 11: Commitment: It's Not What You Think

[42] Pohl, C. (2012). *Living into Community: Cultivating Practices that Sustain Us.* Grand Rapid, MI: William B. Eerdmans Publishing Company.

[43] Meyer, J. (2009). Commitment in a changing world of work. In J. Meyer (Ed.), *Commitment in Organization: Accumulated Wisdom and New Directions.* New York: Routledge/Taylor and Francis Group.

[44] Fisher, A. & Knudsen, D. (1977). *Do converts make the best Protestants?* Paper presented at the meeting of the Society for the Study of Religion.

[45] See Vandenberghe, C. (2009). Organizational commitments. In J.

Meyer (Ed.), *Commitment in Organization: Accumulated Wisdom and New Directions*. New York: Routledge/Taylor and Francis Group; Meyer, J. (2009). Commitment in a changing world of work. In J. Meyer (Ed.), *Commitment in Organization: Accumulated Wisdom and New Directions*. New York: Routledge/Taylor and Francis Group.

[46] Zemke, D. (2010). *Now and Not Yet: The Experience of Tempered Radicals in Christian Congregations*. PhD Dissertation, Gonzaga University.

[47] See Becker, T., Klein, H. and Meyer, J. (2009). Commitment in organizations: Accumulated wisdom and new directions. In J. Meyer (Ed.), *Commitment in Organization: Accumulated Wisdom and New Directions*. New York: Routledge/Taylor and Francis Group; Zondag, H. (2001). Involved, loyal, alienated, and detached: The commitment of pastors. *Pastoral Psychology, 49(4),* 311-323.

Chapter 12: Straddling Two Worlds

[48] The basis for the general description of tempered radicals is based on Meyerson, D. and Scully, M. (1995). Tempered Radicals and the politics of ambivalence and change. *Organizational Science, (6)5,* 585-600. Debra Meyerson has gone on to publish two books on tempered radicals in the workplace.

[49] My PhD dissertation adapted the concept of tempered radicals to change agents in congregations. Since congregations differ markedly from the workplace, how tempered radicals perform within congregations was unknown. See Zemke, D. (2010) *Now and Not Yet: The Experience of Tempered Radicals in Christian Congregations*. PhD dissertation, Gonzaga University. It's also available in the ProQuest database.

[50] See John 4:35, Matthew 9:37-38, and Luke 10:2.

[51] Meyerson and Scully, p. 586.

Chapter 13: Wisdom for Women

[52] Russel, L. (1994). Searching for a church in the round. In M. Winter, A. Lummis, and A. Stokes (Eds.), *Defecting in Place: Women Claiming Responsibility for Their Own Spiritual Lives*. New York: Crossroad.

[53] Bettenhausen, E. (1994). Feminist movement. In M. Winter, A. Lummis, and A. Stokes (Eds.), *Defecting in Place: Women Claiming*

Made in the USA
Coppell, TX
17 June 2021

57541374R00083